One to One

Self-Understanding through Journal Writing

One to One

Christina Baldwin

M. Evans and Company / New York, N.Y. 10017

The quotation on page 165 from the "Little Gidding" section of T. S. Eliot's Four Quartets *is reprinted with the permission of Harcourt Brace Jovanovich, Inc., and Faber and Faber Ltd.*

LIBRARY OF CONGRESS CATALOGING IN PUBLICATION DATA
Baldwin, Christina.
  One to One, self-understanding through journal writing.
  1. Diaries—Therapeutic use. 2. Self-
perception. I. Title.
RC489.D5B34   616.8'916'6   76-58537
ISBN 0–87131–232–8 (casebound)
ISBN 0–87131–294–8 (paperback)

Copyright © 1977 by Christina Baldwin

Design by Joel Schick

Manufactured in the United States of America

9 8 7

For Chrissie,
this is my firstborn, and this one's for us.

Acknowledgments

Several friends tell me acknowledgments in books are silly—but they read them anyway. I hope they read them one more time, for to write a book about the growing process is naturally to draw on many resources, experiences, and relationships. My life is a river of interaction and I hope every person who has stopped to say hello knows that I remember and appreciate their contributions.

There are several people who have specially contributed to the process of writing this book. Ellen O'Neill spent the summer of '76 saying the right thing at the right time. She had an uncanny knack for phoning or dropping by when I was stuck, and her insight and intuition widened my perceptions of the book immeasurably.

Anne Finkelman Ziff picked up the manuscript in third draft when I couldn't perceive it anymore and told me it was good. Her quick editorial comments and friendship became important parts of my East Coast experience.

It was at the Second Annual Women in Writing Conference, Long Island, New York, August 1976 that the process toward publication really took off. The enthusiastic response to the idea of journal writing of more than 150 women, the conference coordination by Hannelore Hahn, and my introduction to Meredith Bernstein, my bright and energetic agent, were just the right crystallizing experiences I needed at the end of that summer's work.

During the revision process, several other people came to my assistance. I want to thank Leo Baldwin for his philosophical contributions and general support, Ariel Hale for her shoulder massages, Sandra Taylor for her artistic visions, and a dozen other friends who telephoned congratulations and encouragement and adapted to my hectic schedule. Karen Mason and Susan Ganoe know why typists always get mentioned: they worked under pressure and deserve much thanks.

All initials used to represent people's names in the included journal entries were drawn haphazardly from alphabet soup. The shared entries of many journal writers have contributed to the growth of the ideas in this book. Through understanding the importance of intimacy to us all, I found the courage to share my intimacy in the journal here.

Writing this book has been an exciting and challenging experiment. I would be glad to know how this experiment works for different readers; what journal ideas we come up with, what new ideas, and what is happening as regards journal writing in different communities. Please feel free to write me, care of M. Evans and Company, Publisher, 216 East 49 St., New York, New York 10017, and include a self-addressed, stamped envelope if you want a reply. Thank you—and good reading and writing to us!

Christina Baldwin

Saint Paul, Minnesota
October 1976

Contents

Introduction: Journal Images

I am a woman whose mind and body fill with the stories of women. My self, other selves. We are looking for each other over the demands of time, husbands and lovers, abortions and babies, housekeeping and officekeeping. Our voices are all high, like sparrows rowed upon the oak's branches. Every morning my counselor's body is a blank page upon which the women come to write the struggles of their lives. Every evening I am filled with journal entries, the scratching of sparrows fallen from trees who write and write their hearts' aching on the pages of the listening counselor mind.

I spend days in a writer's world. I am a writer whose mind and body fill with the Song of Sirens singing in ovarian caves. My self, other selves. I hear stories from the sea bottom, neon-eyed from years of dark swimming where no light penetrates. And I dive for this inheritance whose reality is more fragile than pearls. I dive despite the suffering of my lungs screaming pressure of heavy fathoms. I dive for women's stories and carry them up in my great sea basket, surface with them, line after wriggling line laid out like eels in the sun to dry and sing of the deepest regions. Counselor's world, writer's world. I am the journal.

The journal is a way of connecting. The journal is a connection of the self with the self. The journal sets up an inner dichotomy so that one part may write and one part may read. And since the journal connection between the two parts is interior, it fosters an increased sense of awareness of personal psychology. It becomes a way of observing survival. It becomes an instrument of survival.

Writing journals has become such an intrinsic part of my life I no longer speak of it as something external, something foreign to the rest of my activity. This sense of unity, of the naturalness of journal writing, has grown organically in my life for over fifteen years.

At age fourteen, when I finished reading Anne Frank's *Diary of a Young Girl* and picked up a school notebook to begin my own diary, I had no question of motivation, direction, or duration. I simply loved Anne

Frank, wanted to emulate her, and, like her, recognized, "I want to write, but more than that, I want to bring out all kinds of things that lie buried deep in my heart." "Dear Diary" became my secret place for stuffing notes passed in class, for admitting my crushes and defining that special category of "best friend," for dreaming of myself as a woman, for expressing anger at my parents, and occasionally for cataloging the passage of world events.

But journal writing was not simply a phase of youth. After a brief lapse of writing during college, the rapid changes in living a job-life, ending a love affair, moving, and deciding to leave the country made me yearn again for the sense of someone or something watching. I began to conceive of life as a journey, an evolution of consciousness, and I wanted a way to observe the process in myself. When I picked up the journal again I was still without a sense of form, but with deep awareness of need. My horizons were expanding from those of a college girl to those of a woman, a process so enlightening and scary I wanted to record it from the instant it began to happen. Primarily I needed a companion, someone patient and involved who would never tire of my changing views and location, someone who would shoulder with me the stuff of my life along the way. So I started a new journal, volume one, entitled "At Last There Comes a Journey."

Privately, very privately, the ritual of journal writing grew into my life. Finally I grew ready to share the process. In 1974 when I looked around for a journal vocabulary and writing community and found none, I decided to develop one. I planned and implemented eight-week seminars and workshops in colleges, night schools, women's centers, therapy groups, and church basements as more and more people became interested in their own writings and in writings like their own. This book is the story of my connection to the journal, the development of a process for journal writing, and the sharing of the experiences with other journal writers.

The journal is a river . . . is a mirror . . . is an anchor . . . is myself. . . . The journal is a process of survival.

Considerations for Blank Pages

What Is a Journal and Why Keep One?

A journal is a book of dated entries. The contents may be eclectic, reporting the day's events or one's feelings, dreams, dialogues, fantasies, or drawing sketches, or noting recipes, or quoting from current reading material—whatever the writer wants to leave recorded in her passage through periods of time. The words *diary* and *journal* are sometimes used interchangeably, but traditionally, *diary* connotes a more formal pattern of daily entries, serving primarily to record the writer's activities, experiences and observations. Since the word *journal* is looser in definition, may allow for more creative expansion of the entries, and doesn't imply an obligation to write every day, *journal* will be used consistently throughout this book.

The journal is a tool for recording the process of our lives. There are several assumptions implicit in this process.

The first assumption is that we are capable of having a relationship with our own minds. We are capable of building into our consciousness a point of observation of ourselves. This is not to remove ourselves from involvement with our lives, but is an additional function, a special vantage point. To observe oneself from such a vantage point is not self-dividing; it only acknowledges a many-sided self within the integration of ourselves and makes it possible for one part of ourselves to write and one to read, so that one part may ask and one may answer, one may act and one may reflect, one may explore and one may comprehend the exploration.

The second assumption is that this relationship will be intelligent and basically benevolent. There are many messages fed into each individual's psyche, messages concerning our self-esteem, our expectations of success, our psychological limitations. The dichotomous relationship incorporates these messages, but it also encompasses a higher intelligence, that of life's longing to perpetuate itself and to evolve. I am talking of insight, but also of overview. It is out of this inclusion of overview that the relationship takes on its deepest therapeutic nature.

Theraput originally meant an attendant, or midwife, one who made way for Psyche's head. *Therapy* implies the stretching of one's limbs, or consciousnes, of opening oneself to the imagery and activity of labor. It is the opposite of the word *shrink*. Accepting this origin of the concept of therapy, the therapist is one who attends the labor, and the therapeutic journey becomes an act of birthing. Therapy is a stretching of our birth canal on a mental level. It applies to both women and men as an invitation to let the unconscious come forward into the light of consciousness. In the relationship within our minds, we attend to our labors. We birth ourselves. The journal is the process through which this relationship becomes tangible.

My assumption is that writing makes this connection conscious and helps make possible bringing the unconscious into the conscious. Writing makes this connection viewable, reviewable, and valuable, and grants it a life of its own within our active living. Journal writing is an act of asking the mind for revelation of that which is waiting for attention inside us all. The more we ask of ourselves in the writing process, the more inner labor will occur. As in any relationship, the more we are listened to and responded to, the more we discover what we can share. Trust in the process is grounded in experience, increases through rising expectations and constantly grows with the acceptance of what comes forth.

The last assumption is that this activity is worthwhile, is valid, is, in fact, essential. "Ask and it shall be given you" is the ritual of entry upon which many mind conversations, much personal growth, and the exercises and thoughts of this book are grounded.

What This Book Is About

The main section of this book, The Journal as Therapy, is a series of illustrations that call upon this inner relationship. The illustrations were chosen with the intention of expanding and deepening the awareness with which we approach writing. Though the subjects are presented separately, in the reality of journal writing there is a natural tendency for them to flow together. This is most often the way our minds work, and the topics are only separated out for illustrative purposes.

To ground the processes I describe within a context of journal writing I have included entries from my own journals. In this manner I hope to illustrate not *the* process of growth but provide examples of *one* process of growth. I trust the ability of these selections to communicate because I trust that the intimate does describe the whole. Though the circumstances of our lives may differ greatly, we are all of us, nevertheless, involved in similar life struggles and a similar search for relationship within the mind. The ways I have recorded and reflected upon emotions and experiences in my life may help the reader translate her own writings as they occur in the context of her inner dialogue.

Journal writing is a voyage to the interior. This voyage contains the same elements our lives, thoughts, and feelings contain. The journals will be brilliant—and boring; they will be superficial—and meticulous; they will be humorous—and hazardous. If we are in a state of open exploration and self-acceptance with our lives in general, it will become apparent in our journal writng. Such a state will provide the boundary of the journal and act as a safeguard for the confrontations awaiting us within. The voyage is a venture we may trust, and its intuition will grow with us.

Writing a journal allows us to leave a collection of still lifes that records our personal journeys. The writing process provides space, concentration, and introspection, in which the waiting mind may respond to the asking mind and carry our thoughts further than we could achieve in conversation alone. Using the journal as a therapeutic relationship allows us to stay intimately attached to our own rhythms and patterns of growth. We assume responsibility for our growth and assert our power to deal with our lives.

The honest appraisal inherent in the journal relationship declares a sense of confidence in and understanding of our inner selves. There are times in everyone's life when we lose this confidence temporarily. The journal will not necessarily prevent such occurrences, but it will make a difference in the extent of the loss. The journal's capacity to track down what is happening with our lives increases our sensitivity to our needs.

When there is a problem for which we need outside assistance or protection, insights in the journal can be carried into counseling and used as the basis for work and as a partner in the process of sharing.

Using This Book

This book is written in the first person: I/we. This is the basic voice of the journal. This voice is the language of the circle. The journal relationship is a circle. The circle is the symbol of inclusion, and we are a circle. Involvement with the growth described in this book, the exercises for writing and the relationship we each have to our journals breaks down the concept of author and reader, the idea of one who presents and one who absorbs. This book is a circular process, and, accordingly, we who experience it will translate the "I" into our personal lives and grant it the power to move and affect us. The "I" in this book is not just for me, but for us all.

What Does a Journal Look Like?

There is a little of the fetishist in all of us, and it often emerges while devising the "perfect" journal-keeping arrangement. Arrangements I have seen include three-ring notebooks of varying sizes and decoration, sketch pads, various forms of business-supply materials such as ledgers and steno books, bound blank books, and assorted spiral notebooks. What these various forms have in common is that the writer finds them easy to use and has developed a pattern of writing that is best accommodated by the form chosen. It is not uncommon to experiment with several formats while searching for one that best fits our needs, or to change formats if patterns of writing change.

Personally, I have been using an 8½-by-5½-inch three-ring notebook for the past eight years. I'm devoted to my narrow, orderly lines and to the mobility of chucking an entire volume in my purse or grabbing a few loose pages to carry with me in case of inspiration. When my notebooks get full, or a period of my life feels complete, I bind the pages in a three-ring cardboard cover and stash away another volume in my desk drawer.

Another consideration is the writing instrument. It needs to be an instrument that is easy to use, and leaves a fairly permanent record, and fosters legible penmanship. I have a fetish about fountain pens, which in this age of ballpoints and felt-tip markers has at times complicated my journal writing, but I write most swiftly and unselfconsciously with the free-flowing ink of a fountain pen.

This attention to the physical details of journals and journal writing may sound facetious, but it is meant in earnest. In journal writing we allow ourselves to venture deep into the writing process, and the kind of notebook and writing instrument used can either foster or hinder this process by their convenience and appropriateness. We gain a pleasure that is part of journal keeping when we create a form uniquely our own.

There are many ways to express creativity in the journal. I am constantly delighted with the very particular styles people have developed. One man I know writes his journal in a code he developed himself. And a woman acquaintance of mine writes a journal consisting only of letters, mostly unmailed, to both real and imaginary characters in her life. Another divides her pages into two columns, one objective, one subjective, and writes simultaneous ledgers of what she thinks is happening and what she feels about what is happening. Some people write with a tumbling-out style that doesn't differentiate between real and imaginary dialogues, dreams and daily occurrences, the relationships one is really having with people versus relationships one would like to have with people.

There is only one cardinal rule about what a journal should look like and what style it should be written in: Whatever version works best in the *correct* version.

The Writing Process

There is something about writing it down that is different from talking it out, and it's not just that writing leaves a residue of little black lines on paper. We write things down for safekeeping, to remember them, to honor them. It's a way we take care of our thoughts. Writing is the medium of the journal, and to take seriously the need to *write* a journal we must retouch the power of the writing process.

There is a coordination in the brain among memory, muscular movement and feedback through sight and sound. I do not pretend to understand that process, but I do believe it takes place. The connection began occurring in our brains when we were toddlers and were drawing those squiggly crayon lines and announcing proudly, "These are rabbits' feet around a tree," or "This is a letter to Grandma." We recognized the powerful means to communication in this process although it was not yet in our grasp. I still feel the impact of those early connections.

. . . We are in first grade. Writing is an activity we've been doing for six weeks, and we're getting pretty good at it. Remember? Writing the alphabet, writing our names, writing the numbers up to ten, writing the name of our school. We concentrate so carefully our tongues stick out between our teeth in determination. The letters must be just right, and it's so complicated to keep all the strokes straight in our minds. Each letter is a precise attachment of strokes: circles and straight lines—d–g–p–q–e, straight lines—t–x–z–k–l–w, straight and curved lines—h–r–f–m–n, just curved lines —s–c–j. It's magic.

"Chrissie Chrissie Baldwin Nora School 123456 789 Run Dick run. 2 + 2 = 4 and and and the the the ABCDEFGHIJKLMNOPQRSTUVWXYZ I love you. My name is Chrissie Baldwin." The writing process has begun. It is powerful—even, or perhaps particularly, at this level.

To be able to write and to read was to open our minds to the mantra: I AM. I am, and I feel and I think and I do. I tell you this story and I listen to that story. I want you to know this about me and I want to know that about you. We learned to write, to read, we learned what significance our teachers, parents and other guides placed on those skills, and we became creatures of communication. We were able to send and receive messages in a world far larger than ourselves.

Somewhere in this period of formation some of us were told we were "good writers" and we did more of it so they would tell us again. Others of us were told we were "not very good writers" and we did less of it so they wouldn't remind us. We spent at least twelve years of our younger lives in various states of relationship or rebellion to the writing process. Some of us loved it and got hooked: We write for the fun of it. We write poems and letters and short stories and limericks to be read at cousins' weddings. We write diaries and keep calendars and record dreams and have pen pals. And some of us hated it. After leaving school we found jobs where we wouldn't have to write and ceased writing altogether except for grocery lists and our signatures on checks. We call home every few months so the folks don't worry and tell everyone, "Look, I'm a terrible writer, you don't know how terrible. I'd rather support the phone company than pick up a pen. Look, I'll call you, OK?" And it's such a relief. All sorts of people decide to write journals, no matter what their background, but the anxiety or ease with which we put pen to paper will be different for each of us. We must reacquaint ourselves with the power and magic of writing.

I have always enjoyed writing, but I know this is not universal. When pondering what exactly excites me about writing I came up with the following ideas:

- It's sensual. The side of my hand is an erogenous zone, and to drag it across paper feels good to me.
- It's artistic. The flow of those little black caracters out of my pen is beautiful. And I have cultivated an interesting handwriting because I wanted to be artistic, distinctive, to draw people's eyes to the form of my words and then to the content.
- It's a creative withdrawal. I like an activity to do all by myself in various favorite curled-up positions and in comfortable and serene places

like overstuffed chairs and library stacks. I look busy and people don't interrupt me.

- It's relaxing. I can put something down on paper and relieve the tension of having to remember it. I could never remember everything I want to know, so I store it up, in writing.

When we believe in these light and ordinary aspects of writing it becomes a less awesome process. If I ever got scared of writing I'd go right back to that first-grade level and play with it again. I'd buy some big-lined sheets of school paper and a fat pencil and start writing the alphabet over and over again. Using again these tools of my early years puts me in touch with the excitement they held for me at age six. I even write with my tongue sticking out.

To find out exactly what messages I'm carrying around about writing, I'd remember the scariest or most important teacher I had in grade school, pretend to be her (or him) and start an essay to myself: "Chrissie Baldwin, you should be a better speller. . . . You shouldn't show off by using big words you can't pronounce and don't know the meaning of. . . . You're too young to read that book. . . ." Then I'd go out and buy myself a set of those plastic magnetic alphabets and make big, unpronounceable words on my refrigerator door. I won't worry any more about spelling. I won't worry any more about "full and complete" sentences. I won't worry what anybody is going to think—I will just write for the fun of it.

I start with this sense of graffiti writing from the past and work my way toward the present.

Another way to demystify writing is to see it again as an art form. I'd buy an italic nib pen and a book of alphabet samples and practice calligraphy. I'd turn out beautiful pages of medieval-looking manuscript, even for grocery lists.

When we discover what our inhibitions about writing are, they assume much less power in our lives. If the idea of writing a journal still feels awesome, playing with these and other creative word games will help. Also helpful is actually writing successful journal entries, which build our confidence in our ability to communicate, to reach in and find, to let ourselves hang out on paper.

Flow Writing

Flow writing is the basic form of writing in the journal. It "flows" from the connection between the writing and responding mind. Such writing forms the framework of our connection. It becomes a celebration in words. The content of flow writing carries a full range of feelings, but remains a form of play. To relax and enjoy flow writing, the sense of wonder and fun must remain part of the experience. If the contents of flow writing are more sophisticated than our first mantras, it is only because we have moved beyond the first games. In all the journal entries in this book, even the painful moments, I can look back, become separated from those feelings, and acknowledge my sense of wonder that my mind is capable of such creation.

This appreciation of our creativity is the fun of journal writing. The journal is a place to play with words, ideas, fantasies, mind games. Creativity is the stamp of the individual self, the cohesive thread that binds all our journal work together in a way no one else can duplicate. My favorite image for this comes out of Milne's classic, *Winnie-the-Pooh*. When Winnie-the-Pooh is surrounded by water and in danger of being trapped in the forest with his friend Christopher Robin, Pooh suggests they make their escape by turning Christopher Robin's umbrella upside down and sailing away. They are so impressed by this stroke of genius they name the boat, "The Brain of Pooh."

Many times I have whimsically considered my journal a similar saving grace, and dubbed it, "The Brain of Christina." The Brain of Christina and I flow write many a fancy. In flow writing I approach the journal with nothing particular in mind, settle into an opening image, and let my mind wander wherever it wills while I scribble notes as fast as I can. When we are unaccustomed to using our creative and writing abilities, this process may sound a little frightening: "Suppose I don't think of anything?" Don't worry. You will.

Flow writing is a two-step approach to awareness. First we take a thought, the germ of an idea, and register its presence, become aware of thinking it over. Then we approach the journal with the attitude, it's time to write about such and such, and we write it down—translate it onto paper. Beginning the journal entry we do not know the full scope of our thinking. The flow writing process begins with a statement or question or openness. For example, "I'm thinking about Germany again these days and I don't know why. . . ." Or "What's happening to me now that connects so clearly in my mind with time in Germany?" From this opening, flow writing allows the thoughts to tumble out of us onto the page. Connections are made that we cannot anticipate.

This brings the second aspect of flow writing into play, to use the writing process itself for the emergence of awarenesses. This is not writing down thoughts, but rather allowing thoughts, through writing, to rise up and become verbal expressions. Sometimes we may approach the journal with a sense of need to write, but without any tangible thought in mind. We may start simply categorizing what is currently happening and find the roots of our experiences touching other, much deeper feelings within ourselves.

To find this, I may start writing with a mental image that comes spontaneously to mind. The following example from my journal illustrates this process. It starts with images pulled without conscious concern from the reality of the morning, but moves into a symbolic connection with deeper awarenesses in the psyche.

So cold. Nostrils stick together at the first intake
of frozen air. What I suspect is an old woman
(and not really a bear) lumbers past the house
completely muffed and taking mincing steps along
the icy walk. What I suspect is really a bear (and
not an old woman) follows behind with a red
and hungry eye but cannot catch up. It is 7:45
A.M. and the monster is just the dawn.

I too am red-eyed in the morning, up early
fumbling with the alarm's voice, willing myself to
yes, remember my dreams and no, do not fall
back to sleep. I hold images of airplanes, single
passenger, single engine, that D. and I are flying
over the war zone. I scramble out of my nightshirt
and into a flight suit for reality. Long underwear,
three sweaters, it's a windchill of −20° outside.
The dog whines, impatient to leave lemon icicles
all over the block.

"Airplanes!?" I ask the monster sun, but he has
no reply for night visions. I do not know how to
fly with D. anymore. When our wing-tips brush we
both plummet.

"Come to lunch . . . come to lunch," she calls and
asks me. But what will I say to her except
good-bye? The last time I tried it was so gory, and
she accused me of setting her up in the restaurant
where the ravages of our dying friendship were
a quiet course served with tea. No smoking. No
violence. Japanese cuisine served daily.

Japanese tea—ceremonies again. I can't get away without the ceremonies. It's a choice. The fortune in the cookie says, "Tend to the small stuff." Speak out and you will find the transition does not burn beyond your anxiety of it. Choice: I choose to be free of the weight of not knowing how to care anymore.

Tea leaves in the porcelain cups wash up on either side, visible clusters of the different magnetic poles of her energy going one way, mine another. No, don't slosh the last drop, let the leaves lie separate. What I'm fighting all the time is this careless sloshing together after the leaves have chosen sides, followed the pulling apart of our hands on the teacups. Do not tamper with fate.

Fate? Explain fate, not in Japanese, this is only a restaurant, but in English. Somebody explain to me how everything shifting is still in the pattern of fate.

I listen for my answer, but the words are frozen today. This is, after all, winter in Minnesota, and answers are not forthcoming. . . . Everything is frozen. Hieroglyphs hang on the neighboring elms and the men from the city come and bind them in red, sign their deaths and cut them down. This lack of answers is a disease denuding the city of its promised summer shade. Wait. Wait. Each elm is a message I have not yet read.

My best poem hangs frozen and untranslated in the marked elm before my window. Who will get there first: my mind with its nerve endings of pens, or the city men with great saws and a machine that chews the trees to dust? They are burning this dust at the city borders. Incense hangs over the freeways. At the city's ledge I stand inhaling smoke, filling my lungs with poem ghosts, believing. Nothing is lost. It is fate.

Obviously this entry moves from the playful metaphor of a typical winter morning into a deep psychological statement. There are questions left hanging in a once central relationship, questions of my life changing on levels I cannot truly perceive or control, questions of my survival as a writer. Fate. And I end the statement with the belief that nothing is lost.

I perceive this entry as a sort of psychic grounding within the journal. It shows me a true picture of my disturbance and questioning. This entry is framed by others that deal on a problem-solving level with this relationship, with the changing nature of several relationships in my life that winter, and with my deepest desires to perceive the transitions as they occur. This entry fits in with the rest of the journal picture. I have not stopped to rewrite it or haggle over its spontaneously arising perceptions, but attempt to reread the entry in the same frame of reference in which it was written.

No matter how we approach the mind for awareness, in flow writing there is always the ability to connect instantaneously, in the writing process, with the process of our mind's working.

There is a powerful example of such connection from the life of the sculptor Jacques Lipchitz. In his desire to form sculpture directly from his unconscious, Lipchitz would fill his hands with hot, formless wax and plunge his arms into a tub of ice water. In the seconds before the wax hardened, he would make instant impressions from the power of the unconscious mind, connecting mind to hand. A similar passionate plunging of pen and hand into the mind's waters can occur in flow writing. In a state of receptivity we may write the fleeting impressions of such connections.

There are no external standards through which to judge this experience. Basically we become aware of energy, of the flow of energy as we write, and we learn to trust the process of resonance. Resonance is the idea that the true connection has a recognizable energy or response. We resonate with it. This is not a deep mystical concept, but one that emerges plainly in our everyday experience of journal writing.

To test this point I asked four friends who arrived for supper one evening to grab pen and paper and simply write with me for five minutes. I include all our examples here to show what different routes our minds can take when given permission to run free in writing. Each example not only shows a stamp of personality and creativity, but also illustrates different functions inherent in flow writing.

The old drunk (next door) and his influence on the party group. The old drunk, known to the three local inhabitants as a possibly dangerous pest, spoke in broken words to the two women who were on the porch. Muttering in irregular fashion threatening words about too much noise and calling the police. The old fellow, most likely already living in an alcoholic world of shadow figures and fantasized images, has lost reality to the extent of not being able to tell night from day. Sun shining, he mutters of not being able to sleep.

This paragraph is a launching into story telling. The incident simply struck the writer's mind as an opening image, and she relates it with a particular point of view. Note that it is not all complete sentences, but this does not take away from the paragraph. If anything, it increases the sense of momentum, of its being written from the instant, right from the wax.

He peeks from behind the curtains, that scared little man. His face is twisted with his own self-hate and helplessness. Lace curtains fall around a tired, scarred head. The wrinkles store volumes of puffy ancient tales. This "play dough" part of a man is only a head framed by an aluminum frame that his only relationship to is protection. Fake frames to ease the pain. Fiberglass curtains that imitate lace so one will think of the real. Maroon and gray frames a time when he was young and high jungles of ferns grew on the wallpaper. Wallpaper paste runs in his veins. . . .

The same event happened to intrigue this writer. She starts with story telling, but there is a more emotional interpretation and the paragraph slips into a fantasy perception of the old man's reality. In the writing process, she has started in the instant and found an emotional content that leads her into her own mind games.

"Butter flocks. Flocks butter. Flutterbox Blutter flocks. Flocking butter. Buttery flocks. Buttery locks. Locking butts. Blocking butts. Blocking lots. Letting butts. Betting less. Leasing buts. Beating less. Bleating locks.

"Is it time to quit yet?"

"No."

"Leasing blocks Leaking blots. Slobs, Blobs, Slabs, Blabs, Bleaps, Sleeps, Slops, Blops.

"Is it time to quit yet?"

"No."

Clocks, Locks, Blocks, Socks, Cocks, Knocks, Rocks, Tocs, Wocs, Rocks, oops . . . repeat, roops, spores, pores, doors, whores, roars, soars, snores,

pours, flours, floors, ignores, abhors, adores,
drawers, wars, s'mores . . .
     "Is it time to quit yet?"
     "Yes."

This entry is a singing with words, a mantra of
sound, and, especially with the inclusion of the dialogue, takes on a game-playing quality. The writer is
simply having fun with words, and may or may not
find anything in this singing to reflect on later. Journal
writing need not always be serious business. She has
allowed herself to sit on the front porch and celebrate
her writing game.

Eyes of women. It reminds me how in Africa
they wear symbolic protection at each orifice of
the body, but they don't wear anything on their
eyes. But then, my impression of the eyes of
Africans is of opaque ebony, mirrors which reflect
light only at high noon when the sun is direct,
revealing without shadow.
     I am sitting on the porch with four friends and
wondering about eyes. Our eyes all shades of
brown and hazel hue. My art professor in college
said mouths are the most seductive, that if
people knew how sexy mouths are the puritans
would make us all wear mouth bras. I laughed
then at his perception, suddenly self-conscious for
every tooth.
     But for me—it's eyes. Oh I hope this society

never institutes eye bras. They are such incredible entrance, and I enjoy so deeply their intercourse. . . .

This is an example of writing down the awareness. The writer fixed on an image that had meaning to her and let associated ideas pop into her mind. It is a mind-to-hand process.

Brick wall. Self-discipline. Climbing over, digging through. Weeping, wailing, flailing. Not caring. Caring too much. No iron in the fiber. Glimpses of exhilaration. Jogging, slogging, climbing, slipping.

This is an example of writing with the expectation of images arising from the writing process. The writer takes the image of a brick wall and waits upon it for further insight to come from following the image itself. This one is a hand-to-mind process.

These thoughts are incomplete, since I restricted us to five minutes, but they show our capacity to simply plunge in and find connection. There is no "correct" style to flow writing. We are each capable of all forms, each capable of finding the easiest and most appropriate form to use in our journals, and of spontaneously allowing that form to develop.

To begin journal writing, as either a new or an expanded process in our lives, some time spent enjoying flow writing is good entrance. People tend to decide to keep journals as the result of one of two situations. One is a sort of meandering decision that it's time to organize our thoughts, or bundle together all those scraps of paper where we've been jotting down little notes to ourselves. A second approach arises from crisis, when we suddenly find ourselves pouring out on paper the confusion confronting us. In either case flow writing allows us time to settle into the habit of writing and find the connection that will carry us through so much of the work of the journal. I suggest setting aside half an hour a day for several weeks, just to flow write. After writing, pull back and look at the process until it becomes familiar. Notice the increasing relaxation, enjoy the growth of our minds at play, and observe what patterns of awareness are arising. Most important—celebrate the process, praise the mind for its presents, begin building the dichotomous relationship.

Voices in the Culture

We are journal writers within the context of our culture. Creatures of a very particular making, we need to know the cultural blinders that narrow our world view as well as the psychological blinders that narrow our view of our personal experience. As journal writers setting out to define our relationship to the whole, we are confronted with the forces of the prevailing cultural myths that may challenge the process we have chosen for survival. I wish to mention here two such myths that tend to inhibit journal writing. One is the perception of life as static instead of dynamic. The other is the denial of introspection as a meaningful function in our society.

We are living in a culture that views change as threatening. We are taught to perceive life as linear, implying a destination. Change is perceived as only an intermediary process on our way to this idealized stability. But no matter how we are raised to view life, life *is* change. To see change as the normal condition of life goes directly against the myth of destination, yet meshes more perfectly with experience. When we see change as the normal condition of life we stand in revolt against the expectation of a final goal for our lives and cease to view process as threatening or temporary. To accept change frees us to explore our situation, to define and observe our natural restrictions, and not to be coerced by expectations arising out of society's need for equilibrium.

In light of this culture's view of life as static, it is not out of character that we have invalidated the role of introspection. As long as there were always frontiers before us the compulsion was to tame them. The loss of this physical frontier has left us with a profound sense of containment and limitation. We are unsure how to value the philosophical voices that have survived in the culture, and certainly unsure how to be philosophers ourselves. We are not a question-asking society, but an answer-providing one. The pioneer heritage has not prepared us to become a people with nowhere left to go. But there is still one frontier largely unexplored—ourselves. This is the one our poets and philosophers, our visionaries, have always promised us.

Much of psychology today is the frontier ethic shifted to inner spaces. To make this shift we must accept introspection as a valid function, an integrated part of human experience. As with the territorial frontiers before it, introspection (and psychology) creates its own environment. Introspection begins with the personal, the need to understand the self, then proceeds toward understanding the self in society; and from this grounding approaches an understanding of society itself. Introspection takes the human image from the self to the culture instead of imposing a human image from the culture onto the self.

Journal writing is a tool rising out of introspection. It frames and fashions the course of our exploration. It leaves a record of our journey and a map of entry and return repeated time and again toward our understanding. The journal illuminates the self. And the individual self illuminates the collective self. First we need to perceive the self and then we can perceive the self as a metaphor for the whole.

Our grasp of society becomes translatable through our personal records, our own psychological and spiritual experiences. As we grow to trust the perceptions of ourselves we write down, we grow to trust the perceptions of society we write down. As poet Robert Graves has said, "There is one story only." We are the story and our lives move through the story. In the journal, as we come to understand our personal story, we develop an intuitive intelligence about the nature of human beings that may be translated from the self to the world. We become articulate voices in the midst of change, capable of working from within the dynamic and not against it.

The intelligence that emerges in journal writing is not limited to people of any particular background or education. The voice of the journal writer is the voice of struggle with life's intimate challenges. The voice carries a validity that transcends class, race, sex, age, religion, or income level. These attributes, so long regarded as proper divisions within the culture, become only the framework in which common struggles are recorded.

Validation of the personal voice opens avenues of expression and potential for change far beyond what we previously allowed ourselves to experience or value. Insight will create change that is open to all levels of society. Insight allows us to re-view change and to welcome it into the fabric of our lives.

The Journal as Therapy

THE following pages are devoted to a series of topics and exercises that explore various areas of content in journal writing. They also deal with various areas of self-knowledge. This is no coincidence. To use the journal as therapy means trusting ourselves to use awarenesses gained in counseling, in consciousness raising, or in intelligent and emotional conversations and incorporate them into the writing process. To use the journal as therapy means dipping into the mind for awarenesses to take back into the world, to use in counseling, consciousness raising, and intelligent and emotional conversation. It's a circle, a circle of withdrawal and reentry, retreat and expansion.

There is so much emphasis in our society on "getting fixed," so much dependence on some magical external formula to take care of what's wrong with our lives. The journal is a way of responding independently to our own particular sense of growth, from a viewpoint of ourselves as healthy, evolving human beings.

This self-reliance is especially important for women, who from our earliest years are taught our highest goal —the one behind the social facade of wife/mother—is a throwing away of our psychic strengths. We start as dutiful daughters, giving ourselves away to our parents, nurturing the family structures into which we are born. While still playing with dolls, we are talking about giving ourselves away to a man; by puberty, we are "saving ourselves for our husbands." Later we give up careers for the children or make child raising and housekeeping our career.

This vulnerability is especially important for men, who from their earliest years are taught their highest goal—the one behind the social facade of provider/ husband—is a psychic throwing away of their "weaknesses." They are trained to be receivers of female nurturing, trained to rely on the external magic of competitive careers, male-built social structures, and using rationality as a way to avoid confrontation with their fragility. By age forty they are supposed to have everything "in control."

First we need to go back and pick up those parts of

ourselves that got lost along the way. Then we may redecide how we want to be different, be intimate, be interdependent on each other and society. Both sexes desperately need this process of reappraisal.

When we start reclaiming those parts of ourselves we have been trained to throw away or deny, there is a rush of power we have been quietly hungering after for years. There is also a rush of doubt and indecision, a lack of permission and role models, and a need for communion and community. The journal is a place to tremble and experiment, to build confidence in your individuality without having to seek constant approval from others. We may go through periods of imbalance when we withdraw from intimacy with others to re-establish intimacy with ourselves, when we use the journal as a hiding place for all the terror of redefining our once-solid selfhoods. I accept this. In fact I'm not sure deep change and restructuring can occur without it. But in accepting it I am also determined to have my own growth map within reach—my journal.

Privacy

We all carry around a sense of privacy developed in us through family patterns, the respect or violation of our privacy in the past, trust levels in sharing personal data with others, and self-acceptance of our growing process. It is important in journal writing to become

35

aware of our concepts of privacy and to take care that we provide ourselves with the necessary level of privacy to write freely.

Three things seem to be at issue here. One is to know what our privacy needs are at present and see that they are safeguarded. The next is to examine those privacy needs and seek to understand the motivation behind them. And the third is to decide how we want to handle privacy in the future. To define those privacy issues we may ask ourselves the following questions in the journal:

- What are my feelings about privacy and sharing in general?
- Where did I collect these feelings?
- Do these privacy requirements of my own extend into my regard for the privacy of others?
- Do I make this standard clear in my relationships?
- What do I feel about privacy and my journal?
- Do I communicate my need for privacy regarding the journal to those I need to?
- Who is the "wrongest" person I can imagine reading my journal?
- What is the worst thing that could happen if that person did read it?
- Is this violation still as scary as I've imagined?

If we do not safeguard our present level of privacy in the journal, we will end up consciously or unconsciously censoring what we write, and much of the value of our inner honesty will be sacrificed. Once aware of the importance of our privacy, we can take steps to ensure the journal's privacy in whatever way necessary to free our writing process. We can raise the issues of privacy with housemates or family, communicate how strongly we feel this, and what the consequences are if our request for privacy is violated.

Several couples I know who both keep journals have worked out a code of privacy with regard to their journals. They admit the temptation to peek, may even joke about it, but live by the golden rule. They share from their journals when it is helpful in articulating their private realities as they apply to the couple reality. In this situation the journal is a recognition of the need to protect certain private vulnerabilities. It is also a statement of faith that introspection does not constitute withdrawal, and that they choose voluntarily to return to their involvement with each other.

Of course there are no absolute guarantees. All parties must respect privacy for privacy to be respected. In the hurt and confusion of unhealthy relationships exposure of journal entries has sometimes been disastrous, for instance, in a parent–child relationship or a breaking marriage.

Still, we need to know it is all right to respect and act out our personal level of paranoia. As a teenager I drilled a hole in my diary notebook and padlocked it with my combination gym lock. I hid it in my closet, in the basement, under the bed—moving it occasionally in ritualistic evasive actions. To further protect myself I wrote the most secret parts of the entry in the middle of the page where it couldn't be read even if pried open from above or below. My fierce protection of the journals stemmed from feeling that most of the things I wrote were not settled into myself. Testing my emotions, exploring romantic and sexual feelings, revealing images of myself as a woman, were all too fragile to withstand scrutiny and suspected judgment. I feared that what was most serious and precious to me would be viewed by adults as cute or immature. Since then I have learned that a little more trust of those I love and live with is more valuable. And as I have grown in self-acceptance and enjoyment of myself in evolution I have made peace with the vulnerability of the journals. I am less and less concerned that somebody (this "somebody" usually personified as an authority figure with the power to devastate my self-perceptions) will read what I have been stashing away all these years.

Secrets we put in the journal are parts of ourselves we are not yet comfortable with, or willing to reveal. Perceiving and admitting them on paper is a necessary part of growth. Then as we grow in acceptance through journal writing, these secrets, one by one, become less threatening.

In a roundabout way I have come to see my former need for privacy as a lack of self-acceptance, and my present need for privacy as an understanding of my own vulnerability. I open and close the doors to my privacy out of a sense of respect for what I carry within. I am not afraid of that personal material, but I am aware of my continuing vulnerability to it. I find I have redecided about privacy, wanting to develop my story as fully as possible, and then to simply let it exist as part of the whole. The hinges on my meta-phorical door swing both ways and swing more easily.

Audience and Self-Esteem

To know who or what we perceive as receiving the script of the journal brings into focus our self-percep-tions and expectations. To define our audience we may ask:

- · Who is my audience: Whom do I perceive as listening when I write?
- · Is this listener generally supportive or critical?
- · What are the expectations of the audience re-garding my journal?
- · How do I react to these expectations?
- · How does this affect my journal writing?

In a recent journal workshop "the audience" ap-peared in the following guises:

I write for myself, but I'm very critical. It should be perfect, a work of art.

I write for myself, but oh my spelling. I guess
I'm really writing for Noah Webster, because
I feel haunted by him leaning over my shoulder
itching to make constant corrections.

I write to the future, feeling that long after
I'm dead, women in the future will read this, and
that journals of this century will be valued in
herstory.

I write for my children, things I don't want to
share with them now, but hope they will want
to share of me in the future. When they too are
adults I want them to know me as a woman
more than they can know my adulthood now.

I write to myself, but with a critical sense that
I'm not profound enough. The privacy itself is
intimidating. I feel insecure, and that I'm com-
plaining all the time—like a kid kicking my toe
in the dirt in front of my empty journal. I don't
like the picture that emerges of myself from
this constant haranguing.

I write to my own creativity as a writer, using
the journal like a pantry where I store ideas.
I reach into it whenever I want to work something out on a story or poem level.

There are assumptions, restrictions, and self-imposed

rules of content hidden in each of these statements about audience. None of these is "wrong" but they do affect journal writing and we need to know their implications. What all these statements of audience have in common is a revelation of esteem. The audience personifies self-esteem. Self-esteem is an aspect of the dichotomous relationship in the mind. It operates nonverbally underneath the dialogue just as spiritual aspirations operate nonverbally above the dialogue. Lack of self-esteem is the problem beneath the problems.

From early infancy onward we all incorporate into our lives the messages we receive concerning our self-worth, or lack of self-worth, and this sense of value is to be found beneath our actions and feelings as a tangled network of self-perception. Dealing with, and raising, our level of self-esteem permeates every aspect of journal therapy. The issue needs to be raised at the beginning of writing so that it can be consciously dealt with in the journal.

The form the audience takes is open to evolution in the course of writing, sometimes moving from a very externalized audience to a very internalized sense of what the journal is about. At sixteen I was writing for a male fantasy figure who would come into my life in my twenties and want to know absolutely everything about me. I would love him totally and hand him all my journals. Some people write to a parent, a guru figure, or God. Most often we end up writing to some personalized form of our deepest psychological makeup. In January 1976 I personified my audience in the following way.

I write to myself, to a self that is just ahead of me in evolution—the woman I am becoming today and tomorrow. This new woman carries with her the value system and ethics of the past, as well as what I accept through experience and change. She expects me to be responsible, to be open to growth, and to admit my mistakes, say I am sorry, and learn from them. She expects me to constantly risk moving my life into the next stages of relationships, careers, awareness. This woman is also my friend and mother. She loves me and supports the process I am going through.

I end up seeing myself at age seventy sitting in an overstuffed chair with volumes and volumes of journals piled around my feet. And I will be smiling at all I remember is tucked away on paper, not because it is brilliant, but because its mundaneness communicates my very human experience and my individuality. I expect to have lived the sort of life gentle enough that I may forgive everything.

Such a personification carries both positive and negative attributes. The inner value system that creates and keeps alive such a fantasy figure needs to be consciously recognized. To find this inner value structure, I stop and write a page entitled "Expectations of Myself."

Journal entry: April 1976

MY EXPECTATIONS:

- Be perfect
- Always be sensitive
- Take care of others whenever they need it
- Be loving, gentle, kind, good, responsible
- Be smart
- Be articulate
- Be original
- Be creative
- Be able to synthesize experience at all times, under any conditions
- Be able to cope with experience at all times, under any conditions
- Be trusting and trustworthy
- Be sexually active, and also true to my spiritual-sexual needs
. Be the ideal feminist, Amazon, model woman
- Be open to men, their graceful lover
- Be open to women, their true friend
- Be always full of energy
- Succeed: be a successful writer
  be a successful counselor
  be a successful person

· Be strong
· Keep active
· Have faith

This list is the result of five minutes' pondering, and it's absolutely impossible to live up to. And it's the striving for just those impossible goals, a process that for the most part goes on beneath our consciousness, that keeps us in a state of self-worthlessness. It is the very first item on the list, "be perfect," that governs expectations of all the rest. Not everyone's list looks the same, but they're all made up of so many unattainable goals. Part of the work of the journal is to keep us aware of this list, how it sabotages our feelings of growth and self-esteem, and to step by step erase these expectations and operate our lives from a more humane and accepting relationship to ourselves. When I disgorge this into the journal, it helps me understand why I harangue myself and gives me another chance to release myself from these expectations. This struggle is not only revealed in the journal through list-making, but emerges subtly in various other entries as well. The following one is an example.

Journal entry: 30 July 1975
. . . My ego is something like this July day. In a week of over ninety degree weather, I am moving very slowly not to shake any cell into perspiration. Mentally I am moving very carefully not to shake any cell into anxiety.

44

I am home, writing for the day, and it's been productive. Working on the short story, seeing it near that point of editing, typing, sending off again. . . . By midafternoon I feel foggy headed, very down on myself and ready to telephone friends for some instant positive support. But I stop and try to find out where I am. Where I am is frightening, for basically, down where the worms lie in my guts, there is a lack of self-worth. . . .

I am especially vulnerable to this today, a day when I am living on my own resources, uninter-rupted by the distractions of the job and other people. My self-contempt comes creeping closer and closer to the surface. WHY? I got up this morning, full of sweetness from last evening's visit with friends, got to my desk by 9:00 A.M., finished putting the journal workshop material together by 10:00, and headed energetically into the short story. I am living up to all my reason-able expectations of the day. Why isn't this enough?

Sometimes I feel when I write I should have a friend at my shoulder constantly reassuring me that I am really OK, really a writer, really writing. . . . And I know it is a set-up for me to expect this from another; I need to do it for myself. Speak for myself. But this inner support system is so broken!

If someone I loved came up to me now, laid one finger on me, one finger on that spot of pulsing vulnerability between my brown eyes, I would crumble under that touch like dust. I am like the rose resting on the desk, weeks old, dried in its wine bottle, faded, juices gone, nothing left but a membrane of fragility. It remains whole only until the slightest touch disturbs it. Then it would fall to powder and pollen all over the desk top. We would fall, finally, to dust, because somebody touched and we are too frail.

This entry is evidence of just how deep the self-esteem issue goes. Though I may not have meant to reveal it to myself, the question of self-esteem is a survival issue. And it must be resolved to prevent my, and our, disintegration. Though the audience disappears into the fabric of the journal, it always remains the frame of reference in which we struggle with self-esteem.

Agenda

In the intercourse of journal writing there is an agenda at work that motivates the writing process and provides a framework of topics we are willing and ready to deal with. Both at the onset of journal writing, and in occasional reevaluations of the process, we may assess our current agenda.

- What is my agenda for life right now?
- How am I using the journal in this process?
- What am I waiting to say to myself?
- What am I avoiding saying to myself?
- Why am I, or am I not, writing these things in the journal?

Another way of perceiving one's personal agenda is to look over what does, or does not, appear in writing. I start out by compiling a simple list entitled, "In my journal I write about . . . ," and then check it out by asking:

- Does this list include a full range of emotions, including those I usually push down or forget to celebrate in my excitement?
- Does this list include areas where I am still vulnerable and in the process of change?
- Do I allow myself to appear fully in the journal? (For example, am I humorous as well as serious?)
- Do I forgive myself for past experiences?

What we're dealing with in the question of agenda is a sense of permission. Many times in journal writing we may find ourselves at the end of our inner permission to deal with certain subjects. We carry around little secret rules attached to our concepts about what is acceptable and what is not acceptable for us to feel and experience as individuals. The purpose of assessing the agenda apparent in our journals is to lead us into direct confrontation with the limits of exploration we place on ourselves.

To work on our agenda means to accept this challenge, walk up to our secrets, and work them through in writing the journal. If we look back at the list we just made of topics we write about, by carrying the topics one step further we can see these limits emerge. For example:

- In my journal I can write about what I'm doing with my life; *except when* I confront whether it makes sense or not.
- In my journal I can write about my sexuality; *except when* I uncover questions of how I really feel about my body.
- In my journal I can write about my feelings for X; *except when* these feelings border on hate or rage.

The way these limitations affect writing in the journal becomes obvious when we carry the list yet another step further. For example:

- In my journal I can write about what I'm doing with my life; except when I confront whether any of it makes sense or not. *To avoid this* I never question the basic concept of sense in life.
- In my journal I can write about my sexuality; except when I uncover questions of how I feel about my body. *To avoid this* I talk about my

experiences externally, not how I relate from the core of myself.

· In my journal I can write about my feelings for X; except when these feelings border on hate or rage. *To avoid this* I tone down my feelings, even in writing, and tell myself that admitting them in the journal is enough, I don't have to act on them.

Once we establish a trust relationship to the journal and ourselves, and are comfortable with writing, the journal begins to act as a partner in the process of working through our limitations. It will let us avoid confrontation for a certain length of time, but then suddenly, in the awareness arising from the writing process, our foibles are revealed to us and we must walk them through. New limitations may await our future discovery, but growing confidence in the journal removes their threat, and lessens our anxieties about reaching final solutions.

Memory

Memory is the framework in which our individuality develops, and from our ability to remember all other learning is born. How we remember, what we remember, and why we remember form the most personal map of our individuality. Memory is the foundation

49

of our ability to make use of the process of journal writing. Week by week as we write the journal it becomes a repository of our memories: as true an account of what is happening and our feeling about those happenings as we are willing and able to leave behind us.

Early in her published diaries, Anaïs Nin examines the tendency for memory to mutate, for us to romanticize our personal past. She values the attempt to continue experiencing our lives as they feel in the moment and she assumes our reality is itself more exciting than any fiction we may create around our reality. This concept creates an interesting tension in journal writing.

Very few things about life are empirically true. Events are true: People are born, people die, people get married on a certain day, but none of the feelings attached to such events are *the truth* about them. It is an inhibition in journal writing to imagine we are capable of recording or even thinking *the truth* of an experience or of our lives. Writers may devote more energy worrying about consistency, fairness in recording another person's actions with regard to us, or our objectivity in the midst of decision making, than in acknowledging the importance of our subjective responses. It is necessary to give up the search for empirical truth in journal writing and work from a sense of balance. We can record what we need to record. The flow writing process encourages the natural inclusion of objectivity that is available and valid to us in the moment. We may trust our ability to reach back into our minds and then in the future use the immediacy of the journal's content to refind and re-evaluate what we need.

The record we leave behind us is both one of the more exciting and sometimes one of the more anxiety-provoking aspects of journal writing. Excitement is attached to having a tangible storehouse of our lives; anxiety, to the possibility of perceiving our lives as foolish, resistant to change, or repetitive. But if we have worked out a basic acceptance of the journal and of ourselves, the excitement will outweigh the anxiety.

In the journal's record of memory several levels of life-tracking occur simultaneously. There is the reality of what happens as we experience it, there is the story of what's happening that we share with others, and there is the exploration of awareness we undergo within ourselves. In the journal these three tracks converge, but not so completely that we lose sight of their distinctiveness. Later, reviewing past events, we observe a fourth track: the synthesis of the first three, which explains the meaning in what has happened and how that incident contributes to the present. Without the journal we end up remembering only the fourth track, the synthesis, but not how we reached it.

After major events in our lives a decision-making process naturally occurs, often beneath our conscious-ness, that works toward this resolution. Take, for example, the abrupt end of a relationship. We may experience the following patterns of response: First, the

51

journal records the shock of the experience, the facts, and our reactions. We write straight from our feelings: "Ouch. How could s/he do that to me?" This admitting of an event and the feelings it provokes is followed by a need to share with others, to find some comfort, but also to protect our vulnerability. We shelter ourselves a little from the full force of feeling and the responses of those we talk to. At this point, we talk and write one step removed from feelings: "I told X about the terrible fight Y and I had. I'm really hurting, but it's all right. I'm better off out of that relationship anyway." When we are ready we reexplore the experience by going back to the feeling level. We begin processing the experience out of a desire for comprehension and rebalance: "Yes, I did love her/him, and I couldn't see the ways we were growing apart. I chose to ignore the signs." Here the journal is excruciating—and invaluable. Entries written from the instant record our involvements and do not allow us to deny the importance of our feelings. The relationship as it existed in its heights and depths is written down before us. Eventually we resolve its importance, its termination, its lessons, and are left with an incorporated understanding of this time in our lives. The mellowed synthesis is ready for retelling: "Once, when I was young . . ."

Through resolution we rebalance ourselves and are ready to move on. We need this comfort after the traumas of the past, and experience contentment with our growing consciousness. But the appreciation deepens when we are willing to remember the process, revisit the passion, indignation, hurt, and confusion, and recognize the rests in process we thought were conclusions. By recording and reviewing yesterday's problems we see today's crises as part of tomorrow's story. In writing the journal from the moment, so to speak, we can observe patterns of survival, learn from experience, and celebrate resilience. We acknowledge the risks of involvement and respect the context of our growth. This willingness to reveal our life-tracking permeates every aspect of journal writing and is its basic celebration.

We have "gotten permission" to carry memories with us in large extent from our families, according to how memory was valued when we were children and from the decisions we made ourselves whether or not to remember, for example, things that were painful or discounted by adults, or messages that lowered our self-esteem. We may ask ourselves these questions about memory:

- How far back do I easily remember?
- Were memories treated as important in my family? Did we spend time remembering together?
- Who took major responsibility for carrying family memories? How did that person assume the responsibility?
- How did I fit into the remembering process?
- Were there restrictions about what was acceptable to remember?
- How were such memory taboos enforced?

There is much information packed around the answers to these questions. Our response may be a floodgate, opening us for the first time to the observance of life-tracking. We can record information quickly without stopping to censor or process. Later this raw data is at our disposal in journal work. This primary memory work strikes the tip of the personal and family myth. Personal myth consists of all the stories we tell each other about ourselves. These are most often colored by an unconscious absorption of cultural and family guidelines regarding memory and the responses of others when we have revealed our thoughts and feelings.

To discover the personal myths we carry from our heritage there is a simple consciousness-raising exercise. My mother is an Anderson of Scandinavian-Lutheran background and my father a Baldwin of English-Methodist background. To find the myths I carry from these two groups of people, and how I have incorporated them into my individual history, I simply begin a list entitled "We Andersons are . . ." and another list entitled, "We Baldwins are . . .". The childhood stories of several generations, work and social ethics, concepts of religion and morality, valuation of education and intelligence, sex-role scripting, ideas on the role of the older versus the younger children, and many more little skeletons come popping from the mind's closets in these lists. This material reveals the context in which our memory functions, and points up our personal restrictions and assumptions regarding memory and how life "should be."

Memory is a jigsaw puzzle of incredible minutia. Research psychologists claim our ability to remember early infancy, or even back to the womb. Present scientific theory views the brain as a receiver of stimuli in the form of electrical-impulses which it translates into memories, and that except in cases of cell destruction, these memories are never erased, making even total recall conceivable. However, there is a wide variance in people concerning the depth and range of memory. While science is busy probing the mysteries of our grey matter, we may value memory's function in our growth and enjoy exercising this capacity of our minds.

If we are not satisfied with our recall we may need to ask the mind for memory, give ourselves permission to explore memories beyond the personal myth and simply practice remembering. Occasionally more is needed to break through memory blocks than this gentle process of request and exercise. If we have a memory block not physically based, it is the result of some decision we made not to remember. It may be the result of not valuing memory, or a reaction to specific trauma. Having defined the boundaries of our memory, in this initial journal work we may feel the need to take the journal into counseling and work through the causes for this block. Whatever we find, remember the mind is benevolent and has made decisions out of the need to protect and preserve us. Remember too that those decisions are reversible, as we expand trust in ourselves and provide new contexts of safety for our consciousness.

In the journal we may exercise memory by practicing personal remembrances. We may develop memory by enjoying the tidbits stored inside us and by valuing them.

- What are my first memories of a kitchen? The wallpaper in a special room? The backyard? Paths I knew around the neighborhood? Secret places? Animals and pets?
- What are my first memories of secret things I did and knew I shouldn't tell my parents? Scoldings? Cuts and bruises?
- Do I remember the coming of a sibling?
- What are my first awarenesses of a parent as someone separate and caring for me?
- Starting as far back as possible, I list all my birthdays, or Christmases or Hanukkahs, down to the present, remembering something special about each one.
- I pick the face of a loved person out of my mind and watch the series of still lifes surrounding that image. I write the first impression of that face and the progressions of memory around it.
- Sometimes I go back and try to remember where I was and what I was doing on this date last

year, the year before, the year before that, and so on and on.

The following journal entries show the use of memory in the larger context of journal writing. They were written before I conceptualized the four stages of life-tracking spoken of earlier. Nevertheless, they illustrate this process occurring spontaneously in the journal. They are part of a long-term exploration of my childhood that rambles in and out of the journal just as my memory and past experience ramble in and out of present living and writing. The first entry is a refeeling of original events. It records a time during which I was not keeping a journal, but with guided meditation I am able to effect a sense of these events occurring at the present time. It is also a *story* telling of that time.

Journal entry: 19 February 1974

. . . In a free association session I go back to Indianapolis, to the house on Keystone Avenue and I stay there for an hour reliving all the memories of being five and six years old. This is deeper than memory, this is as close to re-feeling myself as I can go.

There is the yard. How big it is, and I run in the grass and it's always summer. I help my father in the garden and we squat down, talking about brussel sprout buds. I am repulsed and fascinated by tomato worms, they're so horny and squishy. Dad explains everything to me over and over. I step on a bee, feel the sting and cry. My father's arms hold and comfort me. The sound of his voice talking about bees is soothing. I am not listening to the words.

Ahhh, the chicken coop. I love to gather eggs, stooping up and down around the nests. I like the smell of hot shit, hay and hens. The eggs are magically warm in my hands. I have to be careful not to crack them, because only "big girls" are allowed to gather eggs and carry them safely back to Mother in the kitchen. On Saturdays Dad butchers a hen. I am not scared, but the blood is icky. Sometimes the bodies flap off the fence post and run loose around the yard without their heads. My brother chases them, but he's a boy and littler and doesn't know it's not nice to laugh at a chicken just because it's dead. Do I chase them too?

I want to help clean the chickens. I especially like the part with all the tiny unlaid eggs inside. I like to feel the gizzard with all the gravel rolling around in it. I am standing on a chair by my father's side at the kitchen sink. It is hot and steamy in the room because a big pot of water is boiling. We have to dip the chicken in the water and loosen the feathers. I don't like that part. I don't like the feel of the wet sticky feathers.

My parents bought me a bicycle, a squat-tired steel tank, much too big for me. I love it. I ride

with wooden blocks clamped on the pedals
because I am still too short to sit on the seat.
I know where the worst pot-holes are on the
street and try to avoid them. If I bump through
one the bicycle lurches almost out of my control.
I ride around and around our little house.
I don't have permission to go very far.

. . . When the session is over and I am invited
to return to the present, I watch myself jump on
my old bicycle and pedal down Keystone Avenue
into the present. I get bigger and bigger until I
don't need the blocks anymore. I ride swiftly
and with assurance. I pedal into the room, into the
woman body/woman mind of Christina. Ahh, but
do I want to come?

This next entry, written a few days later, carries the
process of memory into the third track. I am now
examining the awareness these memories bring to light,
watching with more consciousness the patterns of my
life evolve.

Journal entry: 21 February 1974
I think my father "got lost" shortly after the time
I describe here. I mean he withdrew emotionally
from the household soon after Indiana. Once
the family transition was made to Minneapolis
he feels not so present. In fact, I remember no
feelings toward either of my parents for several
years, though I'm sure they are hidden some-

where. It is a rather lonely feeling, a sense of always winter. We are trapped together in a fog of familial tension. When I emerge from this unconscious clutter of childhood, I enter into immediate BATTLE with Mother.

Test . . . test . . . retreat . . . withdraw . . . test. I never dare to directly disobey her; I am a good girl. It's something deeper than obedience for which we fight. I struggle to define myself, to withdraw myself from the overwhelming needs and aggression of herself. This may begin at eleven, I think I remember it at twelve. She took me to see the play of Anne Frank and I started my own diary. It was the beginning of consciousness.

I become the kind of adolescent adults like to have around, a good student, serious, questing, sexually inhibited and blushing, even spiritual. If I am a little overbearing in earnestness, I get praised for being articulate.

I am riddled with insecurities by my peers, almost all of whom seem prettier, thinner, more popular, and existing in a perceived solidarity that twists me with doubts at my own convictions.

I counter this scene studying Torah and Japanese, horseback riding, writing diaries and poems, eating chocolate sundaes and making myself throw them up. And every night I spend hours on slowly evolving and replayed fantasies

of my future that go on for months of development.

I am laying the groundwork of myself, and
it is more painful than I knew in the process,
a time I would not choose to revisit despite its
occasional exhilaration.

Later that year, in this second pair of entries, I
have moved the memory process into synthesis. I am
deciding what childhood memories mean to me in the
present. I am dealing both with their power to move
and affect me years later, and with the consequences
of various child perceptions I am still experiencing
as a grown woman.

Journal entry: 6 September 1974
Listen, and I will tell you a fairy tale about
myself as a child. Because I made the mother into
a wicked stepmother, I made the father into
an emperor in new clothes. Because I hated the
wicked stepmother I scrutinized her constantly,
protected myself, battled against her influence.
Because I loved the emperor it was not until this
summer I discarded the armor of my need for
him and perceived a real man/father standing in
his underwear.

New sight. And these days I do not know how
to relate to the emperor's nakedness. Oh, for
several years now I've been able to see and accept

the human frailties of my father, but I have never before risked *feeling* these frailties. It is so new to be angry with him. I don't know how to touch the man who lives in my mind, don't know how or what to think of the childhood camaraderie, the young adult confidences. Our relationship is a string of jewels suddenly fallen off their chain. Some are paste, should be detected and not restrung, but how do I tell which is which without taking the hammer to everything?

Journal entry: 21 September 1974
Waking thoughts: Parental images float loose and alive in me, unattached to time, attached to reality by only the slenderest thread of dreams. Much is lost, time and again, to alarm clocks, the dog's attention, that first clutter of thoughts in other directions, but *still,* I remember my dreams.

Dream: There was a large older house, sort of like Timberlane Road. I was visiting there and it was time for me to go home. Mother put all my clothes in the laundry, got them clean, but wouldn't dry them. She wouldn't help me sort or iron. Dad was watching me and called out questions to Mother such as, "Do you want her to do such and such with the socks?"

Mother would call back in exasperation, "I don't know" or "I'm busy and don't need to be interrupted by such questions!"

The dream reminds me how much we always asked for permission in that house. And to ask was to open ourselves for punishment, to extend our passivity like a child's knuckle for rapping. Dad did this over and over, and she always rapped. And when she rapped *then* he broke out of the passive child and yelled his indignity, his unacceptance of such reprimand. I saw them talk this way a million times. And a million times I copied their conversation.

I wake with all the laundry left to disentangle. Wet beige knee-highs hang in my hands like wilted skins. I am still sorting the dirty clothes of this inheritance. How can I perceive this game of twenty questions, when it was the game itself that taught me to talk?

My father was the seventh child in a strong-lined authoritarian family. There must have been so many people to ask permission from before he felt free to move. My mother was also an eldest daughter, standing just in the shadow of her own parental images. It is a very strong place to stand in the family. They both absorbed too heavily the family burdens of religion, sexuality, pain, and repressed fighting. Now they dole out their burdens again and again and are not free of them.

From my father I learned how to ask. From my mother I learned how to answer. For myself, little self, I was always cringing, skins in hand, awaiting flailing.

Obviously there is more in these entries than memory exercises, but they illustrate the base that memory provides for other aspects of journal therapy. This interrelationship expands throughout journal writing. The need to deal with memory, particularly childhood memories, led me into realization of the next topic.

The Child Within

There is in each of us a continuing presence of the child we once were. In popular psychologies such as Transactional Analysis, "the Child" is given a separate ego state under the theory that this littler being has an outlook of her own and is the source of all feeling responses in the adult personality. Whether or not we subscribe to that view of ourselves, the presence of the inner child remains available and clear.

I uncovered the reality of the child-Chrissie in the midst of looking at childhood memories. Time and again, when opening myself to these memories a connection was made for which I had no understanding or vocabulary. Alone, writing at my desk I experienced myself shrinking, a muscular memory of toddling steps and skinned knees, and an unshakable sense of blond curls turning brown. I reexperienced the physical recording of life from the height of the dining room table. I would feel overwhelmed with a sense of smallness, and vulnerability, but an equally strong sense of determination. Suddenly I hit upon words that began to fit around such feelings.

Journal entry: March 1974
L. was talking to me about her inability to receive, that for her it's a very different function from giving. It feels much scarier, and I asked her why. She said the place in her that gives love is the woman, but the place in her that receives love is the vulnerable child. I say, "It's like a child-hole," and we explore that image until it becomes real to us.

When we needed love as a child we didn't get it, or the love we received was offered in a way that didn't translate to us. Even though we have overlaid years of control between the adult present and the child's hurt past, that need to experience love as shelter is still unmet. Neither of us has dealt with our original sense of hurt and the sense of absence of love. There is an internal vacuum created. When someone loves us in the present it doesn't stay in the adult woman part of us, but gets sucked into the still vulnerable, insatiable needs of the child-hole.

This mechanism occurs in us differently and with differing intensity, but it is a common hole. We have to fill the hole somehow to reestablish our inner balance and integration. How can we make peace with the past? We need to walk our women selves emotionally through the child-hole.

This spontaneous insight was the beginning of long journeying to understand and reunify some of my basic psychological makeup.

In myself, in the women I counsel, and in the friends who have shared their feelings with me this child *hurts. She hurts because it is impossible for any human being to perfectly raise another human being without pain or scar tissue.* I stop a moment to reread that sentence. There are certainly cases of intentional malice toward children, but the vast majority of human beings are raised by parents who are simply doing the best they can, and who were themselves raised by parents who did the best they could, and so back through the generations.

This is mportant to remember not only as we seek the child lost inside us, but also as we remember there are children lost inside our parents, and project our capacities for parenting into the generation before us. *It is impossible for any human being to perfectly raise another human being without pain or scar tissue.* This fact is part of the human condition and needs to be accepted and forgiven and used as the basis for growth. We can work through the child-hole in the safety of the journal. We can express our pent-up feelings because they are important to us and redecide the relationship to our families.

66

We are, at this point in consciousness, at the threshold of an important awareness. We are about to recognize and resume care for our own littler selves. We are now able to stop holding others—past and present—responsible for the child's well-being, and to commit ourselves to direct and caring contact with the inner child. Acceptance of this responsibility will change our attitudes to our emotional lives.

Early in 1975, I had carried the work with childhood memories and recognition of the child-hole as far as I dared to on my own. I took the journal into counseling with me and walked through the connection between Chrissie and Christina. I will share that experience here.

The following entry was written one year after the first entry included in this book on childhood memory, and comes after the process of synthesizing. The speaker in this entry is no longer the woman looking back into the past, but the emotional content of the child-hole beginning to assume a voice of its own. This voice, without being able to identify herself, is really that of the hurting child. I only vaguely perceived this as I entered into counseling.

Journal entry: February 1975
I feel exhausted by my life; by the energy
expended to keep myself together, to keep my
friendships in healthy repair, to keep my head
free enough to write. And I don't know what is
tearing me apart. I look at my parents: my

mother has moved to Alaska, my father is settled into his new marriage, and my godmother's illness rips into me. I dread facing the grief of all this separation. Maybe I am confronting my parentlessness and allowing myself to experience the orphan within for the first time.

I keep up the facade so well. But underneath the facade I am anxious my counselor will send me away, tell me I am not in enough pain to merit her time, and that I will have to gather my psychic belongings and just keep coping. Irrational, but so real to me. I sit staring out the window shaking my head at this pleading girl-self.

My expectation of sporadic, unannounced withdrawal of nurturing, at just the point I am willing to ask for it, feels like a message from the child-hole. How Mother would cut the house dead for hours at a time with all of us tiptoeing out of the way, waiting for thaw. The child-self expects this treatment still. I exhaust myself trying to side-step punishment. I am willing to meet whatever demands I think people may have of me, to anticipate their expectations so they will *have* to love me, so they will not be able to desert me. It is so hard for me to be vulnerable. I come into counseling almost unable to ask for support from anyone. All I hear is my expectation that she will refuse me. I exist as an inner monologue of anxiety.

Journal entry: 7 March 1975

As I get closer to the child-hole the scent of pain rises. Nevertheless, this time I am determined to see myself through. It is not healing to sever myself from the past, to seal off parts of myself that are as real today as they were twenty years ago. I see my sturdy girl-self standing in the child-hole in the shadow of my parents and perceive at last that she needs me. My God, it's Chrissie. . . .

Chrissie, I ran away from you when I was thirteen years old. I almost remember the day I left you off the train with your bloody baggage and shouted "NO! Don't follow me!" And I thought I ran naked into my adolescence without you. And where were you all those years? Left in my guts, quietly trying to sort yourself out, left alone with the demons. No wonder you feel so scared, fearful of survival, easily put under the sway of anyone's demands. Oh, Chrissie, who will care for you if I don't?

For the first time in the journal I have stopped and spoken directly—not to the concept of a child-hole, but to the reality of the child within. Once having invoked her presence, I begin to feel myself from within the feelings of the child, I have experienced the disintegration and may now begin to experiment with integration. The challenge is starkly before me: to accept or not to accept into full consciousness the child's reality and live with the consequences of that reunification in my adult life.

I have this secret left over inside Chrissie. I think if only I am good enough, obedient enough, servile enough then people will have to love me. It's a crazy expectation; that I have some kind of power to make people love me or prevent them from loving me. The child works so hard to compel love, to have affection returned. This is the crux of the child-hole. If I deny this image of personal power, I take the world view of the little person in the child-hole and dump it on her head. Am I ready for that? My counselor hints it is the next step. . . .

Chrissie, the good girl, turns out to be a patsy? I, oldest child, was set up in the marriage to mediate, to assume responsibility for their happiness and the safety of the younger children. But I was duped. I was given no power, the marriage was my parents' game and I was set up to try and try but to NEVER be quite able to fix things, never be able to create family harmony, to win ultimate approval, to feel secure or in control of my own existence. I was fooled.

And I'm sitting here shaking my head and crying, for I ended up doing to Chrissie just what they did to Chrissie, I deserted her. Oh my little wheat-germ girl, I didn't understand. Poor little patsy. Poor Mother, also an oldest unloved daughter. And poor Father, child number seven, picking up all the family emotional garbage. At some time, we were all patsies.

And what to do today? . . . Chrissie, Chrissie, come here. I want to talk with you. I want to hold you on my lap and take care of you, pet you and rock you. You've been strong for so long. Don't worry about this grown-up psychology stuff about being a fool, you only did what you thought you were supposed to do. You just carried out the messages . . . and you were so brave. I remember all the brave and beautiful things you did. I remember your fantasies and your imagination and your pride. I remember your survival and how much love and chatter you poured desperately into your own small world. Let go of my guts, Chrissie, come here. Child-self, I love you. It's OK for us to cry. It's you and me together from now on. Ohhhh, I love you so much—at last.

The reunion of the woman and the child has occurred. I remember this day of reunion even more distinctly than the day of disintegration. Upon finishing this journal entry, I'm sitting and rocking myself and gently crying. There is such a sense of comfort and relief. Chrissie has been waiting over twenty years for it to be safe for her to be young again.

But the story is not over. Probably the story is never over. More than a year later, during another crisis, I wrote the following entry.

Journal entry: June 1976
B. makes a comment in counseling that blows my mind. When B. was three years old and throwing temper tantrums, B.'s grandmother told B.'s mother, "You must take that child and pinion her on your lap until her spirit is broken." But B.'s mother is a modern woman and rejects this obvious confrontation with power. Nevertheless, she, and my mother, found other more subtle ways of tackling their free-spirited eldest daughters. The message was delivered and remains clear, mother to daughter, pinion that child!

Pinion the child to you, to your limitations. Pinion her to accept what life and men will have to offer. Pinion the woman, raise her to accept and chafe under the roles assigned her. Raise her to resent her subservience, but not to free herself from it. Raise her to love angrily, but not be angry. Raise her to throw herself away, and to somewhere hold onto the realization of what she has done. And above all, teach her to pinion her daughter!

NOOOOOOO. Today, I am aware. I am aware, and the chain is broken here. Here, in me, the chain is broken. And it hurts to break a chain inside one's self. Links scatter forcefully away in wreckage. Very tender cherished notions of relationship are shattered in the blow.

And the child who did it—the eleven-year-old brown-eyed inheritor who stood on the rooftop of the family home and asked God, "Would it fix things if I jumped?"—this child stands amazed at the power in her hands. Chrissie looks at the broken links in her hands and sees her hands are too large for her. Chrissie's needs are taken up in Christina's hands: WE broke the chain. A chain that runs through generations, right back across the schooner's crossing, up the gushing fjords to the tribe-like frozen villages of Norway. Pinion that daughter—and today, we broke the chain!

And we stand in the fury of that wounding, catching the blood of it, shard by shard discovering what shall be mended. Amazed and transfixed child in the shadow of her older self —a survivor!

On the other side of the child–adult reunion there is a reintegration possible in which the child-self and the woman-self become shadows of each other. The psyche may now work in coordination of past and present, may take whatever risks are necessary. It is the strength of this union that makes new growth possible. It is the at-one-ment of self that will assert and reassert its healing throughout life. I ponder sometimes the spontaneity of this process, and I am alternately amazed that it occurred at all and frustrated that it took so long for me to articulate the problem and decide what could be done about it.

Everyone's introduction to the child within, greeting point, and reintegration occur differently. The amount of anguish involved in that reunion usually parallels the amount of separation that existed in us between our adult and our child selves. The process of reunion may be consciously aided in several ways.

First there is the groundwork of memory. As I began to experiment with childhood memories, I encouraged the dichotomy, the ability to see Chrissie as a separate being whose history was somehow accidentally an intimate part of me. I placed several photographs of her around the house: Chrissie at age two, Chrissie at eight, Chrissie at fourteen. I sorted through the overlay of feelings about these periods of my life and recorded them in the journal. I tried to work back to impressions of being alive at age two, eight, fourteen. I asked myself the following kinds of questions:

- What do I know about my infancy? Was I bottle or breast fed, demand or schedule fed? How was I touched, how was I cared for?
- What stories and memories do I have of myself as a toddler, including personality traits, specific events, traumas, changes in the family, illness, arrival of siblings? What has been handed down to me as important about this period?

- When do I begin to have independent memories of myself? At what ages of childhood do I see myself and remember clearly? What are the child's dominant feelings at different times? What are her dominant needs? Are these being met? By whom?
- What feelings do I have about this child? How do those feelings correspond to the feelings other family members express about me as a child?
- What happened to me as I entered adolescence? Are there great changes in family structure, specific responses from adults? What were the questions and burdens I was carrying with me from childhood? What did I do with these feelings?

After we have established a sense of identity in the child and an empathy with the child, it is possible to become aware of the child's presence in our adult lives, and perceive the child's voice in the journal. When the journal is written from a state of intense feeling, whether ecstasy or pain, it is the inner child's voice coming through. To write from the child is not to adopt a childish style, slipping into the awkward syntax, careful penmanship, and misspellings of childhood, but to stay inside the feeling and write from there. The child is feeling first and thinking second. The child voice is dramatic, expressive, extreme.

Whether in pain or joy, this child-voice calls out for attention.

Awareness of the child-voice can only increase our consciousness of the child-reality and work toward points of reunion and reintegration. As we become involved in the process of the child-voice we may ask ourselves these questions:

· How do I hear the child-voice in my present life? What is she asking for? From whom does she want response?
· How do I meet the child-self needs?
  How do I ignore the child-self needs?
· How do I behave now that is reminiscent of the way I behaved as a child?
· How does this child feel about her parents?
· How do I as an adult feel about my parents? Out of which state am I reacting to and interacting with my parents? (This question is answerable whether the parents are near or far away, alive or dead.)
· How do I want to change my relationship to this inner child? Where do I find the inner and external support for this process?

At times I have described the reunion of the inner child and the adult as a process of becoming Siamese twins. We rejoin the severed psyches, memories, feelings, and bodies that we had judged somewhere along the line as surgically separable. We learn to act with the expectation of all ourself in coordination. This description is stark, but the reunified self is beautiful, often gentle, and adventuresome.

Once the message has really gotten through, a passage always seems to exist through which the connection can be made and remade without the obstacles that previously blocked it. The journal is an excellent tool for maintaining that connection. And as we achieve a deeper understanding of this dynamic and are better able to write about it, the voice of the inner child becomes ever louder and clearer.

In the winter of 1976, while on a trip to the East Coast, I pushed myself too hard before listening to my feelings and ended up deciding to fly home without completing my itinerary. I needed my own space, and time with my counselor, to safely perceive the crisis I had been avoiding. Familiarity and shelter are conditions that the child sets up to protect herself. The following journal entry is written from that moment of panic when I listened to the child's demand for attention. It is a tumbled flowing of the child needs, the perspective of my whole self responding to those needs, and the decision to stay in touch with them.

Journal entry: 1 January 1976
I would prefer to close this feeling process down,
to be able to continue the trip. But I can't. For
I also want to follow these feelings, to show myself
that I can feel and allow myself to be taken care
of. The scared-child-self desperately wants to

know if this idea about "getting needs met" is just jargon, or really exists. My inner image of myself is a wild-eyed child looking for a place to be safe.

Buffalo airport, flying west toward home: I feel crazy, and I'm scared. This terrified self is pushed to the last defense; crouching child in the farthest corner of my house, crying out for help, to be caught and guided out of here. A labyrinth exists between crouching me and the woman I was yesterday. I remember my other self, sitting at the desk, typing stories, making tea and graceful conversation in the presence of admiring friends. Today she is a stranger who does not glance my way.

If I don't keep telling myself the story of this place will the lady at the desk ever believe me? How will she learn to care for me so I don't flee into the corner afraid and alone?

Some part of me surfaces, discounts this strange reality, gets ready to say blithely, "Oh, it's really nothing. I'm just being dramatic. I'm just being childish. I won't share this. I won't tell anyone about this place. Just relax, it will all go away. See, it's all gone. See?"

No, I don't see. Most of my life I have decided it's better not to speak from this place. Today the pain in here is speaking and I will listen. I cannot escape my own voice sounding nonsense syllables. I am speaking in tongues the groaning of my guts. Three hours to take-off. A circle of cigarette

butts connects me like a life-line to some
forgotten ritual of the desk lady. This time I will
not desert you, my child, I will stay within my
craziness until I know what's happening.

Looking back on such an entry I am impressed with
its rawness and, from the perspective of the desk
lady, a little embarrassed at its drama. Nevertheless,
the voice of the scared child has become an intimate,
accepted, and active partner in my writing and awareness.

Since the child-voice is often expressed as the voice
of feeling in the journal, feelings help us identify
where we are in an overall process of reunification.
Recognizing the split between child and adult is only
one way of perceiving aspects of ourselves that we
have separated and isolated within the psyche. It is a
common experience in our culture to be taught to view
feeling and thinking as separate and mutually exclusive
functions of the mind. Once we have experienced this
dichotomy in the context of a child–adult split, we are
more able to see other areas in which such splitting
off has occurred. The voice of feeling emerges in journal writing without always being consciously indenti-
fiable as that of the inner child. As we become aware
of and examine this voice, the child still aids us by
providing background information concerning when
and why these divisions occurred.

The topics of journal work that follow will raise
questions of feeling and thinking, of child and adult,

of splitting and reuniting. Methods for working through these issues will vary from person to person. The emotional content of child-hole and the way we deal with recent experiences with life-tracking and synthesis affect our perception of surface issue. At this point in journal work, we may trust ourselves in the flow of writing with added confidence that the child is part of our awareness and that we will be able to find her vantage point again and again, whenever it is needed to illuminate the process within us.

Dreams, Twilight Images, and Fantasy

The intercourse the journal sets up in our minds is not limited to rational experiences. Its conversation encompasses the nonrational—as illustrated in the reconnection of child and adult or feeling and thought—as well as the conscious and unconscious minds. The unconscious is commonly brought to our awareness through dreams, twilight images, and fantasy. These messages may be incorporated into the journal and into our conscious growth.

It seems well established in scientific literature that everyone dreams, even though not everyone remembers dreaming. Dreams, like most functions of the mind, respond to attention. If we proclaim, "Me? Nope, never dream," we will assuredly avoid remembering dreams. If we wait passively to see what happens we will only occasionally remember dreams. But if we ask for dreams, prepare to write them down, and later work at interpreting them, we will in fact remember them. This discussion is intended to whet the appetite for dream catching. My statements and ideas regarding dreams are culled from many sources and experiences that have attracted my attention over the journal-writing years.

Dream interpretation has always been a part of mythical and tribal culture. Sigmund Freud reintroduced dream interpretation in terms of modern psychology. His theory was that dreams reveal our most hidden desires, those forbidden sexual and emotional fantasies that are taboo in waking life. Carl Jung's contribution to the understanding of dreams was his discovery of universal symbols appearing in dreams of people all over the world. These symbols come from what he called the "collective unconscious." Dreams from this source usually involve archetypal figures such as the Wise Old Man, the Great Mother, the Inner Friend, and the Anima or Animus, as well as other symbols, images, numbers, and colors that he found to be universally interpretable. Edgar Cayce, a psychic, had dreams that revealed past lives, gave premonitions of the future, warned of illness or revealed its cure, or described astral travel or other occult phenomena. Fritz Perls, the father of Gestalt therapy, emphasized the potential of dreams to work out inner struggle. The recent writings of psychologist Ann Faraday note the great ability in dreams to help us solve problems. And Patricia Garfield provides directions for creative dreaming, in which our waking mind may direct and request certain specific information from our sleeping mind. In the years I have been consciously paying attention to my dreams I have recalled examples of most of the kinds listed above and found them all helpful pieces of knowledge to include in the journal's journey.

Unlike waking thoughts, dreams occurring while we sleep do not leave a memory trace on the brain. For this reason they are most elusive in our memories. To catch dreams we must be gentle with them upon waking and ready to record them almost immediately. Once we have dealt with them consciously they become thoughts and are recorded in the mind as such.

To make sure I catch my dreams, I put my alarm clock (never a disc jockey's voice on a radio-alarm) where I don't have to leap across the room to turn it off, and keep paper and pen right at hand. Upon waking I remain as still as possible and listen to my mind for dream snatches. As soon as an image arises I begin construction around it, even if it's the last or middle part of the dream. Once I have recorded the dream I can later put it into chronological order. Unless there is something in my dreams so compelling that I can't proceed with the day until I've processed the night, I mull the recorded dream images over in my mind until I have time to interpret them.

One of the most effective tools for recalling dreams is simply to start reading about dream work, and to *expect* to remember dreams. If I do not remember dreams as I'd like, I recite to myself before going to sleep, "You are my dreams and I have a right to you. I will remember you, treat your messages with respect, and explore further." Then I date the paper by my bed and, confident, fall asleep.

Once I have a dream to work with I follow a pattern of inquiry developed by combining selections from Ann Faraday's work, parts of my own training in Gestalt, and a background of intuitive responses accumulated from years of recording my own dreams.

The first thing to trust when I want to explore the symbolism in a dream is the idea of resonance. This concept, as defined in Faraday's writing, states simply that the correct interpretation of symbols will resonate, or ring true, as we discover it in ourselves. References in dream books may list the interpretation of symbols, but I do not accept that interpretation until I have tested it against my own resonance.

Including dreams and dream interpretation into the journal may be handled in many different ways; note the dreams included in the entries on flow writing and childhood memory. In the flow writing sample, brief reference was made to a dream within the context of the entry. Dreaming the unsettled nature of my relationship to D. introduced into the entry the reality of the night as it was affecting the reality of the day. In the synthesis-of-memory entry the dream is included as a metaphor for the psychological reality with which I am struggling. In both cases the meanings of the

83

dreams were so obvious to me I did not have to stop and interpret them, but simply included their immediate importance into waking journal work.

If the meaning of a dream is not so immediately obvious a little ritual can be performed, which often cracks open its meaning. I repeat the dream aloud to myself several times, always telling it in the present tense, until I am back in touch with the action and symbolism of the dream experience. After that, I ask myself a few basic dream questions:

- Why am I dreaming this dream now?
- Are there symbols in the dream whose interpretation is obvious to me?
- Are there symbols in the dream that I remember from other dreams?
- Are there symbols that reflect my activities, my interactions, or even the television programs I've seen during the last few days?
- Are there any puns in the dream?

In January of 1976, while still in the midst of resolving the crisis that had brought me home from the East Coast and back into counseling, I had the following dream. In retelling it, I hit upon one symbol for understanding the whole dream. Here is how I recorded the dream in my journal.

Journal entry: 7 January, dream date,
10 January, dream interpretation

For some reason I decide to go back to Plymouth
[where I grew up] and find my horse Taffy. I
am at the Oak View Lane house pulling the dusty
saddle and tack off its hook in the garage. Taffy
is older too. I am aware that much time has passed
since I was last here doing this. I feel a little
nervous about saddling up, feel a little creaky
once I am mounted.

I ride the dirt roads behind Beacon Heights
Elementary School. It is warm, no distinct season.
There is a dump yard at the bottom of one hill.
I ride toward it, lead Taffy into it, dismount and
start rummaging around, curious to see what
might be in here.

As I am poking around, a large white garbage
truck pulls up on the rise above the dump yard. A
trashman gets out. The truck disgorges its
contents. Pieces of fresh garbage are falling all
around me. I see the new leather journal I took
on the trip east come tumbling down. I try to
reach it, notice it has been slashed in half. I go
up the hill and meet the trashman in a large
lavatory. The lavatory is the kind found in parks
or roadside rest stops. We talk and he tells me
what it means for him to be a trashman. I have lost
the details of this conversation, but I am
interested and comfortable with the man.

Notes on the dream: Taffy is the key! In the despair of last Tuesday, I said to [my counselor] that I had to give up the dreams I had of myself as a girl. Taffy symbolizes the dreams I had of myself then: freedom, flight and control. I am one with the horse's back, feel her power between my thighs and her response to my guidance. We are always taking off down the back roads, in and out of secret places. Ahh, I reveled in the romance. I ride her into the sunset, sneak out to the pasture at midnight to lie naked on her shoulders. She is freedom and I am strong woman-child.

And we arrive at the dump, that out-of-the-way place where everything eventually ends up needing to be sorted through. It's a comfortable old dump; I am expecting to find antique bottles, not fresh garbage. But along comes the white truck—white is feminine in my mind. The truck is female, womb-like and grinding gears, bearing new contents for my dump. Down comes all the fresh garbage, the surprise crisis of the new year. And in among the other ruins is my new journal, the one I just began as I headed east. The journal is in the dump, discarded. I don't have to keep holding onto this pain and confusion. It's been broken through, may now be discarded, allowed to mellow from rotting garbage into an artifact.

And the trashman is friendly. A man, he represents rationality, animus, thinking processes.

86

I meet him in the lavatory, which is where one goes to get rid of shit. In this environment I chat with him easily, respond to the information he gives me about his function and role. I am glad he is in charge of the truck, that he gathers the garbage, and leaves it where the sun (light of consciousness) can dry it, and does not bury it. It all seems a very natural unoffensive process.

I wake with a feeling that I am in good hands, may trust my own processing of this crisis. I may reclaim the image of myself that was born riding Taffy, and see the recent helpless angry self-image in the journal as something which needs dumping and resolving, not that which ought to govern my life from this point on.

This example of the dream in journal work is more complete than any previous examples. Here the entry focuses directly on the dream, and my interpretation makes specific reference to the experince I am living through. Beginning with my interpreting the horse image, the dream's message flows from the unconscious to the conscious. The notes, not strictly analytical, slip the dream into the context of the crisis currently being recorded elsewhere in the journal, and the dream is integrated into my conscious awareness.

As we delve more and more seriously into dreams and attempt to interpret them, we will most likely be confronted with dreams that resonate as important but that do not reveal themselves easily to us. When necessary I will go through a dream symbol by symbol until I understand it. The following dream took some detailed work to unravel. I recorded it in the present tense and read it aloud three times.

Journal entry: October 1975
I am walking my dog [named Pope] a few blocks from my house—the neighborhood looks realistic —when a huge male lion runs in front of me and up a big tree. The lion looks just like Pope would look chasing a squirrel. Though I am walking the regular dog route, I notice then that Pope is not along. I am frightened by the sudden appearance of the lion, but glad Pope isn't here for fear he and the lion would get into a fight. A huge squirrel, as big and fierce as the lion, follows the lion right up the tree, as though to protect the smaller squirrel the lion is chasing. Neither animal has a tail. They circle the tree trunk, chasing each other round and round, and disappear into the tree's foliage.
I am standing by some bushes, but sense the bushes aren't much protection. The lion comes down out of the tree, looks me straight in the eye and lopes off. The big squirrel is out of the tree too and I notice it has a wound in its right rear hip, but doesn't seem mortally injured.
I begin making my way home through the neighborhood alleys—now the scene is no longer

realistic. Every house has a dog out on a chain. Some are friendly, some are barking fiercely. I am walking through a maze of dog runs—like wire cages and dogs on yard chains.

I come to Mrs. Jennings's house. A friendly middle-aged man is raking in the alley. He says to me, "Oh, hi. I asked Mrs. Jennings about the fenced yard (it seems I had previously inquired how she put up the fence for her dog), and she says it's easy and the best thing she ever did for the dog."

Mrs. Jennings is sitting on her porch. She is a strange woman, about thirty years old, sloppy looking, a housewife who likes country western music and soap operas. She calls out to me, "Yah, I really love that fence." I go up to her porch. The porch is a mess, with the TV turned on and some bland daytime show making background noise to our conversation. Mrs. Jennings has a very passive four-year-old girl curled on her lap and she is feeding her pudding. There is also an animated, smart, dark-haired girl off to my left side sitting at the breakfast bar on the porch feeding herself. While I am aware of the dark child, I never look directly at her. This child talks like a real four-year-old, while the blond one is just like a vegetable.

The dream dissolves into a scene in my kitchen. I. (a close friend), G. (a therapist), and I are discussing the price of the fence. I say, "It will cost $84.47." G. says, "That's expensive."

I wake up.

The dream was a puzzle to me. It didn't remind me of any dream I'd worked on previously. When I asked the dream questions the only resonance I found was that the lion equals strength, and that the lack of tails indicates the animals are symbols for human characteristics. This was not interpretation enough for me to understand the dream, so I proceeded through the dream, symbol by symbol, asking each one, "Who are you and what are you doing in my dream?" Sometimes I do this in Gestalt form, using what is called the "empty chair" technique. "I" sit in one chair, or on a pillow, and "place" each symbol on an opposite chair or pillow. After asking the symbol my question, I switch pillows and assume the place and consciousness of the symbol and answer from the symbol's point of view. For example:

ME: "Neighborhood, who are you and what are you doing in my dream?" Switching pillows, I sit a moment until I *feel* like the neighborhood, and answer myself with whatever response floats freely into mind.

NEIGHBORHOOD: "I am your real environment, and in your dream I tell you this is really happening."

Using this technique I came up with the following "answers" as to the meanings of my dream symbols:

The dog, Pope: "I am your responsibility; I depend on your care."

90

My chore, dog walking:	"I tell you that you're still carrying responsibility around, not finding ways to leave it at home."
The lion:	"I am your strength."
The little squirrel:	"I am caution."
The huge squirrel:	"I am caution to the extreme."
The tree:	"I lift things from the ground up into consciousness."
The wound of the huge squirrel:	"I am wounded by extreme caution, and my wound is on the right (the rational) side because I think too much."
The alleys:	"I am the back way home, your mind, and no longer the external environment."
The dogs on chains and in yards:	"We show that everybody has responsibility, and everybody has to find some kind of boundary for it."
The man in the alley:	"I am a father figure in your mind, and I tell you there is a rational response to responsibility."

The fence:	"I am a boundary on responsibility."
Mrs. Jennings:	"I am your shadow side, everything about being a thirty-year-old woman you are not, the negative feelings you have of yourself."
Mrs. Jennings's appreciation of the fence:	"You think I take the lazy way out of assuming responsibility, and that if you get 'a fence' you'll be like me."
The blond child:	"I am passivity, and can't do a thing for myself. I will grow up to be like my mother."
The brunette child:	"I am independence, I make up my own mind, and am active and bright. I will grow up like you. Listen to me."
I. and G.:	"We are your support group and want you to decide what to do."
G.'s comment, "That's expensive.":	"I recognize that changing your attitude toward responsibility is risky (costly)."

Now I have all the pieces to retell the dream with its symbolism revealed. I fit the pieces back into context by asking why I am dreaming this dream now and come up with the answer, "I am having this dream because I am dealing with responsibility throughout my life right now. The dream clarifies the issue and my fears in dealing with it and offers me a direct challenge to change." Now that I understand the dream, I can get a glimpse of my sense of direction by saying the dream once more in the present tense, this time ending it any way I would like.

In this sample dream there are two figures I interpret in Jungian terms, the "shadow," represented by Mrs. Jennings, and the "wise old man," represented by the man in the alley. Becoming acquainted and friendly with these inner archetypes has given me a sense that I am not alone in the house of myself, that there is a coordinated intelligence working to increase my inner understanding. There are Jungian psychologists who have devoted their whole lifetime to understanding the role of archetypes and the collective unconscious. Rather than attempt to encapsulate such knowledge in a few paragraphs, I suggest reading books in the field and have included some of them in the bibliography.

Another aspect of the mind's fancy that is as interpretable and titillating as dreams is twilight imagery. Twilight is that state just before or after sleep when the door to the unconscious mind is still ajar. Until we are accustomed to twilight images they are often more fragile than dreams. I discovered my mind's twilight imaging in two ways.

In simple yoga meditation, that is, holding the mind still, not repeating a mantra, images would rise after a period of mental calm. The following journal entry records a meditation image.

> I am watching something come out of depth, a
> spinning ball-like object, tumbling bright blur
> rushing toward the point of view of my con-
> sciousness. It suddenly stops. It is my body not
> as I am, but as I am not, sitting in lotus position.
> It steadies itself from the ride, as though a little
> dizzy, sitting with hands placed for balance
> on a rough wooden floor. I become aware of myself
> in the body, look up and smile, aware of myself
> in my consciousness, watching. I shake my head
> as though to explain something, and with a few
> unsteady movements rise and walk away.

The second way I achieved awareness of twilight images came from watching my presleep images. I learned from Ann Faraday that I could find twilight images by lying in bed on my back with an arm raised, resting on its elbow. When I am drifting almost to sleep the muscles in the arm relax to the point where the arm will flop down, hitting my body. This awakens me just enough to capture the images floating through

94

my mind in this state. The following is a record of a twilight image:

A stage, like for a beauty contest, with light bulbs shining in rows along the platform. Out parades a line of male figures, but they are made of chrome, all smooth rounded shiny metal without features. As if on signal they halt, and brilliant rays of light shoot off from their chrome genitals. The scene is repeated, but the figures now are all female with the same chrome bodies and lack of feature. As if on signal they halt and there is a flash of light shooting from them. The beams shoot not only from their genitals, but also from breasts and mouths and foreheads. The scene vanishes.

There may be more consciousness in these visions than in dreaming, but they originate with the same spontaneity from the unconscious mind and are delivered to the conscious mind as gifts. Our role is simply to accept them and to assume a receiving posture in as many states of consciousness as possible. Like dreams, these images respond to attention and interpretation, and their variety can be tested through resonance.

Another form of fantasy is what we commonly call daydreaming. While it is presently popular to admit to interpreting dreams, no similar emphasis has popularized interpretation of waking fantasy. We tend to consider these fantasies more consciously controlled and hold ourselves responsible for their content much more than for that of dreams. We continue daydreaming in a secret, slightly embarrassed Walter Mitty fashion and admit our daydreams to no one, perhaps not even ourselves. Writing down waking fantasies in the journal and admitting to their intention, importance, or symbolic content may teach us a great deal about the connection between the conscious and unconscious mind. It is also a way of fostering inner dialogue and pulling back into one vantage point or another for a look at our lives.

Through acceptance of day fantasies and looking at the patterns developed in them across time I learn a great deal about my self-image and expectations.

As a girl it was my habit to fantasy myself to sleep each night, knowing it would take one or two hours to relinquish myself from daydreams to night dreams. Innocent of recognizing any psychological implications the fantasies might have, I looked forward to that secret special time. And since they are waking fantasies their recall is within memory:

> *Age 5:* I am Annie Oakley, riding a beautiful horse all over the Wild West, and I make friends with cowboys and Indians.
>
> *Age 7:* I am a famous woman doctor who is given special children to raise because I am the only one who can understand and cure them. (I remember

that this fantasy stemmed from feeling my dolls were not real enough, and that only I knew they were *really* real.)

Age 14: I am living on a plantation in the South Pacific with a handsome husband and five beautiful, bright children. I am an attractive, gracious woman who writes books about our ideal lives.

Age 17: I am working in the Middle East as director of UNICEF, and run orphanages. I fall in love with a dashing Arab who reminds me of Kahlil Gibran, and live a life of foreign service and glamour.

Age 23: I am living in Salzburg, Austria, where I find a wise old man to initiate me into all the wisdom he's learned and from whose friendship I emerge as a wise young woman.

Age 27: I am hurt in a freak accident which leaves me mute for one year, during which time I am forced to write everything I want to share with people. The journals and novels of this period become best-sellers and I become an incredibly spiritual and mature person, a romanticized Helen Keller.

Once these little novels of myself were my most carefully guarded secret. They were protected from the scrutiny of the journal-writing process—lives that I never wrote down, talked about, or shared with other people. But I find them now, slowly emerging into writing and tucked into recent journals without comment or explanation as though by simply writing them down I perceived what I needed to know. When I was ready to include them in the journal, I was ready to work them through, almost as I would work with dreams, and accept the messages that emerged.

Within the above list, for instance, I see definite, consistent images appearing. I see a child turning into a woman who always expected life to include adventure, risks, responsible tasks, and romance. I am amazed and delighted to find roots of my present independence in Chrissie's adventures as Annie Oakley. Also present, even at this age, are some of the social values that later develop into fantasies of working for UNICEF. In adolescence when I attached myself to a romantic man and to wife and mother roles, I retained expectations of my individual success. As my experience with romance and careers became something I lived out and fantasied on a different level, the epic fantasies of my twenties turn to the business of spiritual transformation. I enter periods of hoping for a transforming experience, the tutelage of a guru, or a time of trial that will rid my life of triviality and produce the idealistic person I want to be.

I firmly believe that some of the adventure that really occurred to me in my twenties—moving from Minneapolis to other major cities, to Europe and Israel, and moving from the gentle limitations of a midwestern girlhood into a much more liberated womanhood—were possible because I began imagining myself capable of such experience, years ahead of their reality. And when I turned over my life directions to fantasies of external guidance, the person who was more like a guru to me than anyone else appeared in a dream and declined the role. He informed me, "The days become months and the months become years and that is the pattern." It was shortly after this message that I became increasingly aware of how I used these fantasies, and understood the expectations hidden within their adventures. I accepted life as a series of small but significant moments and ceased longing for inspirational shortcuts.

This is not to deny the value of these fantasies. They are all in the right path—each expressing positive alternatives and need for growth, and providing a way of thinking myself into the future, defining and redefining myself. I consider them friends, remember them fondly, look them up in the journal and in my mind, and revisit their reality like occasional vacations.

These epic images of ourselves in the world are not the only way people fantasy. There is a part of the mind I call the "inner movies," which almost constantly makes use of fantasy. Watching an old woman walk down the street, I may detect the inner movies playing a complete fantasy run-through of her life. Sharing a plane seat beside a stranger I may fantasy what version of myself—or what completely fabricated story—I would tell him. Meeting a person I am strongly attracted to, I may chat brightly in greeting conversation while the inner movies play out the entire potential scope of our relationship, even to the point of naming children, or grieving at the termination of our affair. When I am in the doldrums I spice up my life with some fantasy of saving grace—a new career, the chance to travel, a new relationship, some astounding insight.

This creative tripping, and carrot-before-the-horse aspect of the mind, is part of fantasy's natural function. Science is proving fantasy essential to a person's creativity, stability, and ability to be introspective. We need to accept the adventures and foibles of our daydreaming with at least as much tolerance and respect as our night dreaming. We need to celebrate these mental extensions of ourselves and our lives, and acknowledge their uniqueness. We need worry about them only when we find ourselves turning away from reality to live in fantasy, or when the contents of the fantasy frighten us, or when we can no longer tell the difference between fantasy and reality.

So far the dreams and fantasies discussed have been largely spontaneous. But there is also a way to construct fantasy at will. One of the points in life where such fantasy construction is useful is in decision making. Ira Progoff, in his work with what he calls the "intensive journal," terms confrontations with decisions "decision intersections." He recognizes that for every decision made in life there is an alternative not chosen and theorizes that fantasying is a useful way of consciously exploring those rejected alternatives, to settle business left over from past decisions as well as to guide present decisions.

When I find myself thinking, "If only I had done this . . . ," or "If only I hadn't done that . . . ," I explore in fantasy the opposite side of my chosen reality. We are constantly at these intersections in life. Upon meeting someone we seek out or withdraw from increased contact with them, we decide to marry or not to marry, to have children or not to have children, to pursue one career or another, to travel or stay at home. Exploring the curiosity attached to these options will free us to regard options differently in the future.

This fantasy of will, or fantasy of option, consists of two elements: (1) allowing ourselves to imagine life as it would have been if the opposite decision had been made at any given time, and (2) stepping into fantasy to help you make a new decision.

Permitting ourselves to fantasy the opposites, or unchosen alternatives, of our life's chosen reality may be risky. Suppose I fantasy that I did marry R. in my midtwenties, and suppose I end up wishing I had, and suppose I decide my intersection choice was second best. What then? Then I have more journal exploration to do. The function of such fantasy is not to make us unhappy with reality, but to reveal the context in which we have made, and are making, life decisions. It is a way of grounding ourselves firmly into the context of our own personal lives so that we can eventually accept the decisions we've made. Looking again at the example of R., I recognize the circumstances that prompted me to act as I did. Fantasy offers me the chance to reexamine those circumstances and make a new kind of peace with my behavior and with what has developed in my life as a result.

I have an image of myself called "the lady of the scar tissue." This is the woman I have become in the labyrinth of choices made. It is a positive imagine, in which I celebrate the full range of experience and emotion that has brought me to this pont in life. In the journal I can work through this process without embarrassment or hurt to others.

I also go into fantasies of option when confronted with a new intersection in life and feel the need to understand its implications and potential consequences. This is the second element of this kind of fantasying. In this technique I freely fantasy myself in a situation, incorporating in it anything I want, then ask:

- What expectations emerge about this event?
- What is the best thing that can happen?
- What is the worst thing that can happen?
- What kind of time, space, and sense of commitment do I realistically have in my life to follow the path of this decision?
- What will have to fade out of my life if I follow this new path?
- Am I willing to take the risk, and what will support me in either path?

And these questions provide a bridge from the fantasy back to reality.

102

In the journal I am working in a context of many options, and such fantasy work reflects other currents of journal work. At this point, discussion of dreams and fantasies has led us solidly back to reality, to our work with the conscious mind. It also provides a basis for examining the subjects taken up in the next two sections.

Friendship

Friendship has no civil, and few emotional, rights in our society. We all talk of wanting friends, and talk about the friends we have, but there is little acknowledgment of friendship's importance that helps us define, protect, or commit ourselves to friendship. In friendship we face the risk of realizing nothing can really be demanded of another person. The relationships that are most valued in our society—husband–wife, parent–child, even employer–employee—are all legally binding contracts in which certain responses are anticipated. And if the proper responses are not forthcoming, the contract may be broken and the relationship (at least the obligations of the relationship) terminated. This assumption about relationships encourages us to also assume that only legalized relationships are truly valid. The implications of this for friendship are horrendous, for despite romanticized concepts of comradeship, friendship falls outside societal codification. Since society prefers to honor legal relationships, people may undervalue friendships. We may escape some moral dilemmas this way, but in doing so we miss a realm of human expression different from anything we will learn elsewhere.

Friendship provides a kind of constant feedback on our state of being that is different from the response we receive from our family. When we talk to parents we know they envision us as babies, children, and fledgling adults as well as the person before them. When we talk to spouses they envision the passion of early courting, the nervousness of new marriage or parenthood, and tremulous expectations of shared old age. Friendship provides a kind of pipeline to the present, a meeting over and over again in the present tense. I think part of this ability stems from friendship's nonlegal status. If every time we saw good friends we remembered all the little wrongs we had done each other it would be almost impossible to proclaim this free-will affection. So we meet in the present, grateful for this inexplicable gift.

Friendships also provide a support group—people who will see us through crises by perceiving from the outside what we can't see from the inside. They love us and are almost as concerned about the outcome as we are ourselves. And through friendship we often experience risks of sharing that make possible greater vulnerability in the family and in our personal growth, knowing we have communicated and survived within the shelter of friends.

104

Fortunately some of the consciousness raising that has occurred in the women's movement has raised the question of friendship also, and challenged us to widen and deepen our circles of trust. Yet despite this obvious need for recognition of the value of nonblood and nonromantic relationships, few of us have contemplated how to maintain and revere current friendships, let alone approached others openly intending to share new friendship with them.

Dealing with the issue of friendship in the journal I can scrutinize my relations with people without being either too vulnerable or critical. It gives me a chance to write both the philosophy and actuality of my relationships. It reflects my belief that I *do* create friendships and *can* create them to fit closely to my needs for sharing and support. I began this exploration by asking:

· What does the word *friend* mean to me?
· With whom am I friends?
· What are my criteria for making a friend?
· Are the criteria the same for men and women, and how does this affect my approach to people?
· I list all my friends:
    What am I getting from each person?
    What am I giving to each person?
    What am I not getting from friends?
    What am I not giving to friends?
    Why?

What ideas do I have about changing this situation if it doesn't satisfy me?

Besides making this appraisal of our friendships, it is valuable to write about friendships themselves. Though it is frustrating, after a rich evening of talk, to try to record in the journal the essence of what was said, it will leave us a skeleton of the evening's content and feeling. From this skeleton we can see patterns that help answer the questions about the giving and receiving that occurs between ourselves and others. And if the relationship runs into trouble, we have a way of checking out our interactions and looking for the nonverbal emotional interactions upon which the friendship is really based.

In the journal we become aware of inner realities of friendship. There is the outer reality consisting of shared experiences, conversations, and feelings. And there is also the friendship as it occurs inwardly: the little things we cherish privately about our friends— but also the potentially dangerous myths of the relationships. These myths consist of secrets like: This person is my guru, this person is the "best friend" for whom I've been searching, this person is a potential lover. And if these expectations are not met—which is highly likely since they are never brought out into the open—we feel inexplicably let down. We act out of these myths whether or not they are consciously recognized. But if we are conscious of them their potential danger to us is lessened. Journal writing helps bring these expectations to light and helps us examine and deal with them.

It is scary sometimes. We are conditioned to guess what another person's expectations are, but not to ask directly. We are conditioned to believe that someone who loves us should be able to guess what our expectations are and therefore we don't need to state them. But after working with friendships in the journal it is easier to risk directness and thereby clarify the bonding.

And all this work brings us back to the original sense of risk. A good friend once said to me, "There are no guarantees. I want you to have what you need for yourself, but I also want me to have what I need for myself. If we can provide this side by side, wonderful. . . . I hope so." The idea that someone who loved me would state so unsentimentally the transitory nature of relationships was terrifying. But I eventually realized how right she was, and that all the talk in the world about never parting and never letting anything come between us was just armor against this simple reality. There are no guarantees.

Once we accept that, it is a most freeing concept. Love . . . and do what you will. If we are free of the mythical armor of expectation and permanence, we can let the relationship and the reality of the other person be free. And if we are free we are far more likely to remain side by side journeying together. In my personal experience, the price for learning this lesson has been painful, but so is the price for never learning it. I have simply made the choice to experience the pain consciously, and to work again and again at understanding myself in relation to others.

The following journal entries illustrate the skeleton left in writing about one friendship. This friendship has been a growing toward consciousness that has not always been clear or easy. There has been constant tension between the full, imperfect personhoods of M. and me, and between the myths of friendship in each of us that needed recognition. We started knowing each other in a time of transition and crisis in other relationships. Our needs for someone to represent stability and shelter are obvious in the first entry.

Journal entry: July 1974

This evening M. was here and we drank a bottle of wine, sitting on the couch talking and touching. I continue to be humbled, grateful, and astounded at our friendship.

There is nothing I feel protective about between us—not that we sit down to say everything we've ever known about ourselves, but we speak from the freedom implicit in knowing there is no withholding. She therefore helps me stay in closer contact with my emotions and my self.

I keep trying to think if I have ever experienced this before, and then wonder why I am concerned with finding some past familiarity upon which to ground this. Enjoy the present. In this relationship I am not "in control" because there is no

"control." We are both grounded in similar under-
standings of self and loving and responsibility.
While I love her I don't see myself projecting "the
inner friend" image upon her because she is
so real-ly herself. Whatever trips I tend to lay
over her she displaces with the gentle durability
of her self.

I am letting loose this love in me and I am a
little afraid. More than any other person in my
life right now I see M. with a future flowing
out ahead of this present. It may be a messy
redundant struggle, but I want to keep trying to
articulate this relationship, keep learning to say
the experience.

Shortly after this entry the relationship is confronted
with a change in our accustomed patterns of being
together. The consequences of these time changes are
recorded in the journal.

Journal entry: October 1974
I see M. almost every day. She stops by for tea
in the morning, or we take a late evening study
break, and we talk on the phone. But I feel our
"time" has just disappeared into law school
and her man traumas. I am frustrated at how to
get her to be a good friend to me. I need her. I
want her to be around in some real way.

We are good friends. I love her and she knows it.
She loves me and I know it. But there's so

little time! One of the things I look forward to about our Christmas California trip is seeing her again without the book of Torts in her arms. And having admitted all this to myself, and to her this evening on the phone, it becomes livable again. After listening to myself talking with her, I decided I'm becoming stilted in the way I approach her for time, for energy, or the way I behave when we are together. I've stopped expecting her full attention or to be able to finish a conversation to its resolution.

I don't like what this does to us, to her feelings or mine. So I'll try to be spontaneous and assume she can, and will, exercise her right to interrupt, to make and break plans, to come along or stay and study, to put in and withdraw energy according to her needs. We have to exercise the equality we both ostensibly feel in our friendship. She's laboring under a false guilt trip for ignoring me. I'm laboring under a false passivity trip trying not to step on her time and energy. Enough of that for both of us.

Such honesty goes so against our training, it is always experimental, full of hard lessons.

It is now three years since I first met M. and we have run the gamut from business associates to best friends, from high spontaneous greetings to totally self-conscious conversations of pain. At times I have almost ceased writing in the journal about this relationship with the excuse that I just don't know what else there is to say. But the relationship continues and its recording continues.

Through this struggle we have acknowledged the civil and emotional rights of friendship. We have held up for review the expectations that bond us unconsciously together. It is still not easy, but it is easier. We have raised our consciousness of each other and our trust. We celebrate the effects of this growth, both within our own relationship and in the other important relationships in our lives. Our friendship is recorded in the journal where I can review the lessons learned and work directly from the process of intimacy with another person.

Time Structuring and Problem Solving

We are trained to function within society in roles assigned us by cultural expectation and economic efficiency but that may or may not have anything to do with our individual needs. But we need to be able to define our tasks and to experience a sense of personal control over our lives if we are to function fully as human beings. The lack of fulfilling tasks or the loss of control over time can literally drive us mad. These elements, along with food, shelter, and emotional nurturing, are basic survival needs. When our confidence is shaken in our ability to solve problems and

111

control our time, depression results. It is necessary to deal with the role depression plays in this situation for depression makes us passive and stands in the way of our ability to change.

Depression is not a feeling itself, but rather a means of pushing down our true feelings. It's a psychic defense system, acting to protect us from issues we are not yet ready or willing to face. Depression coats the area of rawness and soothes the mind while hiding the cause. And as long as it is tolerable we tend to cope with it as the problem instead of with the problems that are creating it. To look at time structure and problem solving in our lives is to take the risk that we may no longer be satisfied with our daily patterns, that we may need to change. But when we have been depressed long enough, we usually rise up angry, ready to fight our way out no matter what the risk.

To do that we must know what is bothering us and what options are available for changing our lives. For this reason problem solving and time structuring are combined in this topic, though certanly not all problems are directly associable to time.

Time Structure

Our society urges all of us to throw time away. It stupefies us in a soothing plastic environment full of material prizes. And because most of us are content at some level to drift along in days full of tasks we

do not particularly enjoy and haven't consciously decided to do, we feel anxious that weekends and vacations be perfect, that activities and associations become
meaningful on demand, for this is our only real time.
As we face the realization of how much of ourselves
we have given away we need to ask ourselves two
questions: What exactly are we doing with our days?
And is that what we want to be doing?

To consciously observe our use of time for one day
is a revealing step to opening dialogue between time
and our needs. I observed a day of time by carrying
a small pad and pen with me everywhere and jotting
down, detail by detail, absolutely everything I did,
from rising to retiring. Later I compiled this into log
form in the journal and used it as the basis for review
of time. It brought to light not only the varied activities
of a typical day, but also where time was available to
me that I hadn't seen before.

How much time do we spend in the bathroom every
day? How much time is spent preparing, eating, and
cleaning up after meals? How much time during an
average day are we on the telephone? How much
time every day do we spend wandering aimlessly
around the house or office looking for some task or
other activity to strike our mood? How much time is
spent shopping when we have just gone out for milk
and bread but are entranced by all the visual come-ons
of the shopping center?

As we look at this pattern of time, we also discover
our feelings about time. Emotional responses are in-

herent in every moment. We are making decisions constantly about the next moment, the next hour. Most of our decisions are so automatic that we don't perceive the process except in those situations where we have to "make up our minds." Once we have looked over this broad pattern and started recognizing the feelings and automatic responses we have developed, we can begin becoming more and more conscious of time as structure. What we are telling ourselves about our use of time, and what we are experiencing in our use of time, may be very divergent realities. To become more aware of what is really happening to our time, we may spend a week including this daily exercise in the journal. Every morning when I wake up I list:

- · What do I have to do today?
- · What do I want to do today?
- · What do I predict about the way my day will go?

Every evening I stop and record:

- · What happened to my day?
- · What got done that I had to do, that I wanted to do?
- · What is building up from yesterday's list that will have to be dealt with tomorrow?
- · How did I handle control of time over my day?
- · Did I make active and conscious decisions about time? How or how not?

One day in the spring of 1976, my list looked like this:

114

Morning list:

· What do I have to do today?
Go to work at the women's center, attend staff meeting, do counseling all afternoon, teach a journal class this evening.

· What do I want to do today?
Be centered in counseling sessions, have some time to myself, catch up with my own journal writing, have time to relax with friends.

· What do I predict about the way my day will go?
I will get the "have to's" done, but I am more tired than I want to be. I just want to counsel and not deal with administration problems, but don't know how to create this for myself.

Evening list:

· What happened to my day?
I got through it as predicted, but had to ignore my own energy rhythms. I had a surprisingly good journal session, when my energy returned as I needed it.

· What got done today from my list?
One therapy group, one fairly mellow staff meeting, two counseling sessions, a journal class, an hour of late evening privacy with classical music and sherry.

· What's building up from yesterday's list to be dealt with tomorrow?
My own journal writing, planning for the next

journal course, my continuing needs to relax and share more support with friends.

· How did I handle control of time over my day? I have little sense of control over time. I shut the office door and did a few minutes of yoga breathing, but I'm pushing myself hard.

· Did I make active and conscious decisions about time?
Somewhat: I said NO at least three times today to requests for future commitment. I paid attention to the almost overload situation in which I'm working. But I let other people intrude on my privacy at the office, using our exchange as a substitute for my need to center—a tenuous "high."

This journal entry, which began the week of reckoning with time, briefly illustrates the mental framework I was in when the list was made. There is a vulnerability here which is not treated lightly. From both the list and the following entry floats a sense that this work in the journal may shake my time patterning to its foundations.

Journal entry: April 1976
Sun streaming in the living room windows before I am even up, plants all translucent in the glow.
It is an April Monday. I sit at the desk reading morning devotions and realize the day, despite sunshine, is opaque before me. I have no particular

reason to hesitate before it, but I have no sense of it yet: therapy group, counseling, talking with the other counselors and friends. I experience a certain fluttering of mind into list making, culling order. Sometimes I wake with clouds in my head, anger, or depression, any overview of the process lost in my personal fog. But this morning is neither high nor angry, just a sense of waiting in the sun for my own green translucency to appear. Beginnings are sometimes as shaky as spring in April. . . ."

These entries are from a time when I was "at work," and they reflect the need to preserve my sense of self in the midst of outside environments. Not everybody's day bears any resemblance to the specifics logged here. Everybody works, but we do not define everybody's work similarly.

In our society there are two distinct life-styles of time structure. We call them "being at home" and "being at work." And unless it's Saturday, when everybody's supposed to "be at home," the idea of work, as defined by an external business association, is more highly valued. Housewives and mothers, as many of them are trying to convince us, WORK. Retired persons, as many of them are trying to tell us, WORK and want to continue working. As we assume conscious control of our activities, time structure assumes meaning and value, no matter what the tasks involved or what the environment in which we spend the day. All time structures lead us into patterns of unconscious response and need our review.

The broad question of how we view and value work in this society is not the main subject in the journal work here, though it certainly needs our reappraisal. But revolution begins at home, begins with our willingness to assert control in our own lives. If we really allow ourselves to pay attention to our use of time and follow through with changes in attitude and activity as necessary, that is revolution enough for today.

The philosophy that emerges from the exercises given here is reflected in many other aspects of journal writing as well. Assuming responsibility for the way we spend our lives is also a matter of self-esteem, a matter of support, a matter of our inner child's needs as well as our adult needs. When in the midst of appraising our use of time it is helpful to remember three slogans:

- This is not a pass/fail test.
- There is humor in here somewhere; LAUGH.
- Celebrate something about each and every day.

To further clarify my needs regarding time, I fantasy. At the end of a work week, I fantasy what it would ideally have looked like.

- What are the hours, the tasks, the interrelationships of people, the environment, the support, the power structure?

- Confronted with reality what can I do to bring my situation closer to the ideal?
- Is this level of change possible?

I fantasy an ideal free day.

- How do I spend time? With whom?
- What are the backdrops, activities, entertainments, food, weather?
- What can I do now to incorporate some of this fantasy into my own free time?

From such fantasies we can begin to assume more control over our lives and the pleasures available to us. We can design periods of private celebration for ourselves every day: dancing to the stereo, yoga exercises, finger-painting, napping, reading a novel in a long hot bath, eating in bed—whatever strikes our fancies. We literally resume control of our time structure minute by minute. We have a growing sense of assurance as our worlds do not fall apart in response to these assertions over time.

Co-workers accept easily the closing of our office doors, or the crusade for a private secretarial lounge, or our choosing to play tennis instead of drinking after work. Families learn to cope when parents read a book in the evenings, disappear into the darkroom, or take off for a day in the woods alone. Friends continue to telephone even if we can't go to the movies three requests in a row, or admit we hate fishing, or change our minds and ask to spend an evening alone.

119

As we experiment with our ability to maintain control over our daily lives we move into problem solving in the journal from a stance of personal power.

Problem Solving

Often we will realize *something* is bothering us long before we know exactly *what* is bothering us. In the journal we leave hints, record depressions, admit to minor and major quandaries. Sometimes we get so far into this meandering we can't see the issue anymore. We need to stop and ask directly, "What is bothering me?" Many times the simple act of asking will bring an answer to mind. And if we do not answer ourselves immediately the process of reviewing entries and probing for clarification may lead us into direct confrontation with the mind's ability to keep secrets.

When a problem deals with parts of ourselves, our time, or our involvement with other people that we are hesitant to change, the mind may protect us from confrontation by obscuring the issues from us. Examples of this phenomenon tend to appear in journals over the course of long writing. We know, and cease to know, important bits of data as befits our needs of the moment. Sometimes this hesitancy needs to be included in the rhythm with which we approach our personal growth and change. And sometimes it needs to be challenged, made conscious, and dealt with swiftly.

Years ago I fell in love with a man already married.

In my journal I laboriously examined my perceptions of him, of myself, of our capacity to endure the strain of romantic involvement. In the course of this writing I decided he would never leave his wife, that his sense of honor could not sustain both relationships, and that I did not want to be isolated in the position of "other woman." I decided against the affair and continued journal lectures at myself to withdraw. However, our attraction grew and we spent the next three years entangling and disentangling our lives. Once our course of action was determined I "forgot" these early perceptions, came to expect his divorce, and was stunned at the outcome of our involvement. The journals faithfully record my changing view of reality and expectation. They are full of secrets I was keeping from myself. Even as I reviewed them during this time I still didn't register their content except as it supported our present course. Now, with regained objectivity, the foibles of that period are most obvious to me.

If I had been more aware of my capacity to obscure my own honesty I might have provided both of us with a clearer understanding of our involvement, and myself with a better sense of perspective in the process of reassembling my life. Now whenever I am deeply involved, in a relationship, in my work, or in emotional change, I can approach the journal with a practiced eye. I read it in search of the inner honesty no one else can give me, and which I may not know I've already given myself.

Once we experience a confrontation with our secrets, our patterns for protecting them become clearer and we learn to draw honesty from the journal. Secrets are largely a matter of keeping track of all our options. Secrets develop because we decide (consciously or unconsciously) that some things about an issue are too scary to look at. So we bury them. We forget them, and build our consideration of the problem and its solutions on top of the hidden secrets, pretending they don't exist. We all have something about ourselves or our situations that at first thought we consider intolerable. To suggest what these might be, I'll stop and list such things under the heading, "I couldn't stand it if . . ."

. . . I found out I was illegitimate.
. . . Henry left me.
. . . I got to be sixty and my career didn't make sense.

These thoughts are the secret fears we hide away in our minds and hope never to see again. We may construct the decisions of decades around such hidden suspicions. What is intolerable about these secrets is not the fact of them, but the power we give them by assuming they are intolerable. The journal provides a place for us to uncover our secrets, admit them to ourselves, deal with our reactions, and ground ourselves in a reality that includes them. If we still have trouble dealing with them the journal provides a framework for carrying our secrets into a counseling relationship.

To work on problem solving in the journal it is first important we know whether or not such secrets are involved. Our personal secrets may hang like roots beneath far simpler problems. For example, a woman came for counseling when she was having trouble with her manfriend. Everyday tensions of miscommunication were the superficial problem focus, and she was questioning her level of commitment to this relationship. Much fear seemed to be attached to her perception of the problem, and one day in the middle of a session I asked her bluntly, "What's the secret?"

She blurted out, "My mother always told me I'd grow up to be a dyke, and now this relationship is falling apart, so I must be gay!" From then on we began looking at the problem with the secrets revealed and were able to consider all the options. Once she had admitted her fear of this prophecy the problem's resolution was much simpler for her.

When confronted with a problem we can clarify in the journal, we need to ask for it in context:

- What are the possible secrets, restrictions, or taboos connected to this problem?
- Have I experienced a variation of this problem before? How did I handle it then? Does that solution still seem appropriate to me?
- Is there unfinished business left over from pre-

vious experience that influences the way I feel now? How must I deal with that material from the past?

When we understand the context of the problem, we can ask for practical understanding:

- What are my priorities for fixing this problem?
- What are my possible alternative solutions?
- What are the consequences of each solution? How do they feel emotionally?
- Are my expectations for working through this problem realistic?
- Am I blocking movement by insisting on the ideal instead of accepting what is really possible for me now?
- Considering all this information, what feels most appropriate for me to do?
- What kind of commitment will this take?
- What kind of time will this take?
- Assuming I am ready to take action, what resources do I have that will support me and help me solve this problem?
- Where do I need additional information, guidance, or support?
- Do I know how and where to get that assistance?

I have found, both in my own life and in counseling, that we do not make changes unless we have accomplished two things: We must have prepared *interior acceptance* for change to occur, and we must have provided *internal and external support systems* for making change. This is where much of the previous and ongoing work of the journal becomes so valuable. Through the journal we are in a state of dialogue with ourselves, able to reveal the full contents of decisions, learning how to carve out interior acceptance for change, and providing for our support. These are not fantastic claims for the cures of journal writing, but reasonable expectations of the dichotomous relationship.

The following entries present an example of how a problem wove its way through several months of my journal writing and contain many of the elements discussed in the sections on both time structure and problem solving.

For some writers the shorthand approach of question asking and list making is very comfortable. For others the straight narrative is the most accustomed style. I present this particular problem for illustration as an example of the way question asking and techniques for problem solving can be used in the journal without including any lists. Analysis of the emotional content in these entries makes use of problem solving techniques without application of any strict format.

In March 1975 I had been freelancing for over a year and felt stuck in the slots available to local writers. I wasn't supporting myself financially, and that pressure was shaking both my sense of skill and my emotional equilibrium. I decided I needed more structure, more money, and more involvement with people. A job opening as community planner for the city's Bicentennial Commission offered me about eighteen months of organized activity and steady income. I took the job with relief and promised myself to keep writing on the weekends. I had time structure, money, and a supportive atmosphere where my talents were recognized. By the middle of May I was writing:

> *Journal entry: May 1975*
> It's Sunday evening. I've been running through the paces for weeks and weeks and suddenly I have a chance to stop and catch my breath—and that means I have to figure out what to do. I'm really just beginning to realize what it means to be tied into an office/work structure for the next eighteen months. I miss my writing, and I admit I really won't make the commitment to arrange writing time while I am working 40 hours a week. I don't know if I'll be able to stand that. The trouble is, writing is engrained in my self-image and ego strength, and when I don't write I don't accept that I am not writing, but instead expect more and more of myself. I get into an angry placating stance against my own expectations.

The first contexts of the problem are being exposed. I have taken on a demanding job that I find unsatisfying, despite its supportive atmosphere. I am focused on the loss of previous activity and former time structure, which, now that I have little chance to use it, appears even more valid and important to me than before. I remain emotionally invested in writing as my primary activity.

In July I am still bargaining with myself for more time. By staying focused on this external issue, I avoid dealing with the lack of fulfillment in my present time structure. The following entry is superficial, chatty; I am not concentrating on inner feelings.

11 July 1975

Friday—Friday. How sorry I am sometimes to find
my life so definitely divided into weeks and
days. It's going to be a long year. And yet there's
a relief watching the calendar pass from June to
July: Next year at this time it will all be over. I
will be writing thank you's, finishing up the
bills and the details, rehashing last-minute Fourth
of July traumas and beginning to laugh at it
all. I look forward to laughing my way out of the
Bicentennial and into my own freedom again.
Two hundred years of freedom—I can take it.

This next entry is the first one to deal with the emotional importance of the issues. It reveals the secrets. I'm running into a personal taboo: It is not "responsible" to give up tasks midway through a commitment. The assumption of responsibility is an engrained personal value I am just beginning to question. That sense of responsibility has shown up in problems I've experienced before, and it's obvious that material from past confrontations and expectations is affecting the present.

16 July 1975

D. walked in this evening, looked me over and announced, "My instant analysis of the situation is that you're feeling trapped by the Bicentennial, sorry you ever took the job, angry at your misjudgment, down on yourself for not writing and feeling like you don't have any space."

I laughed and offered her 5¢ for being right on. Then I told her my fantasy: I spend hours imagining a crisis that will precipitate a way out of this job commitment. I imagine a bike accident some morning when I am flying downhill toward the office, even being attacked in the alley while walking the dog. If this happens it will have several consequences: (1) I won't have to go to work; (2) I can plead that the crisis has rearranged my priorities and they will understand and not demand my return; (3) I will have that lovely convalescence in which to write madly all day long; and (4) such a traumatic experience will of course bring me once again closer to personal enlightenment.

D. whistles in astonishment. "Look at how severely you are willing to punish yourself simply

for wanting to give up that job! Look what
you're saying you'd have to suffer before seeing
that as a reasonable option. Do you really mean
that? What's the worst thing that could happen
if you went to your boss and told her you'd made
a mistake, and won't do this with the next year
of your life?"

There's a long pause while my stomach turns
over. "Well," I say, "the worst thing that could
happen is that R. wouldn't like me anymore, and
I'd have to live with making a mistake."

"Do you really mean to give R. all that power
over you?"

"No, I'm not really fighting her. I'm listening to
all the 'good girl' tapes inside myself, especially
one that says: be RESPONSIBLE, stick by your
decisions, always carry through, bear up to your
responsibilities and expect others to do the same."

I go around and around on this responsibility
issue. What about the job? What about the
parent tapes? How much responsibility should I
take? Who or what is making up my mind?
What about my friends and my support?

I decide to tell R. I don't think there are 40
hours of work for me in this summer's slack
time, and that I will take a pay cut and work
fewer hours until the fall. I cannot function
with this enforced office idleness which keeps me
away from home, from writing and from my
real self.

I continue to view writing as my primary pursuit and find the financial trade-off of the Bicentennial job too high a price for separating me from this activity. The issues are being clarified as the taboo or secret level is exposed in the journal. I am into the momentum of the problem, but not yet accepting the change internally. By the end of these entries I better understand the dynamics in what is occurring, but am still not ready to risk movement. I decide to solve the problem by bettering my relationship to it, but not by getting out of that relationship.

Also it is obvious that the two ingredients for change are still missing. I do not have an idea of what I'd do instead of this job, other than return to the vaguely defined poverty of writing, nor have I found other support to counterbalance the parental/ethical messages on responsibility. Though I don't, by any means, have this problem figured out, the entries reveal a willingness to carry on a dialogue with myself, explore the issues, and seek alternatives.

At the point when change is decided, where action is the next step, the consequences of making the change must be faced and resolved. If secrets have been hiding in the decision, they tend to surface now all at once at our most vulnerable point. I have learned to expect them, and that helps remove most of their terror, but not always my surprise. In the last moments of dealing with the issue the fear in the inner child becomes even more apparent. I have resolved to quit my job, despite the inner expectations concerning responsibility. This is a step of new assertiveness, an experiment that tests the strength of both new and old patterns of behavior.

4 November 1975

I wake from dreams of clashing metal. The dog
barks reveille, and I find the River Rubicon
lapping on the mattress shores. And I, Caesar,
with my resignation letter in hand, take decisive
action toward new paths. It is accomplished,
it is accomplished, all but the final announcement
to the office staff. My bravado does not survive
the day. . . .
I have been so depressed. Days of meetings and
planning for a future I have already deserted
are too hard. I am afraid still of R.'s reactions. I
anticipate my relief, I can feel my freedom
swelling within me, recognized after last month's
struggle. At the office I am all nerves, but at
home I am a new self, waiting for my daring
disobedience to end this job. There is such a
frightened child in me who awaits punishment—
but there is an equally strong natural woman
who claims my right to change my mind. They
are tearing me apart. Mail the letter, Christina,
mail the letter.

6 November 1975

A day of good office work, sharing the last day of
camaraderie, secretly knowing my resignation

will arrive tomorrow and life will be quite different.

R. and I ride the bus home together chatting of tasks. My tension grows. She gets off a stop ahead of me and walks home to my letter. I walk the dog counseling myself in extreme anxiety: "Christina, this is just what you have to walk through to be on your way." I ride it out.

7 November 1975

Guess what . . . she laughed. She smiled, she hugged me and we had the most comfortable chat about my resignation. R. was extremely complimentary of my role in the office, and offered to let me continue half-time. And not once did she make me feel guilty or coerce me; she understood and sympathized with the long and painful process this must have been for me. She even said my resignation letter was beautifully written! And I talked with her easily, not adapting, not afraid, not feeling any pressure to conform to her idea of working half-time. I've spent the day slowly coming down off my tension, shaking my head and realizing the anxiety is over and that it was all in my mind.

Now I need to explore further what it is in me that is so terrified when I assert myself. And I am telephoning all my patient friends who have seen me through these past weeks and telling them it's over.

One thing I appreciate in this particular process of problem solving is the confusion of emotional material revealed through a situation that "should be" simple. It teaches me to respect and search out the underlying emotional assumptions in my actions. It resolves one instance with the beginning of another search. It includes my need to celebrate and states my intention to know more.

The journal is like that—we finish an entry, but never the book.

Sensuality and Sexuality

We talk a lot about sensuality and sexuality in this culture. We openly express a great range of yearning and experience. It is popular to speak a vocabulary of sexual expertise and to hide the frustrations and questions we experience in our physical relationships. It is popular to rally around sexual freedom and ignore the resulting tangle of commitment and confusion in our life-styles. The quieter aspects of our physical sensitivity to life and the environment, let alone the subtler gestures of love, get lost in the rush to be "supersexual."

Supersexual is a term based on performance, not on enjoyment. It denies us a full range of physical response to the world. I suggest we replace this term with the concept of being "omnisexual." Omnisexuality

133

allows us to experience a sensual/sexual connection between ourselves and the world. It allows an easy flow of feeling for men and women, for the chairs we sit on, for the breeze filtering through our clothes, for the water showering our nude bodies, for the taste of food we eat. Omnisexuality is experienced through the sense of open channels between our personal life energy and the energies around us. We may learn to trust this flow of energy, to sense its appropriateness, and to redefine our needs and limitations. I suspect we have much to learn, and unlearn, before we can approach life with such spontaneous appreciation. For without knowing it, we are acting under many assumptions, which we can hardly perceive, much less examine, through the blinders of our ethics and training.

One assumption, implicit in our language itself, is the existence of the words *sensual* and *sexual*. It sees physical sensation as divided according to appropriate intent, "physical" response as different from "erotic" response. It is acceptable for us to feel *sensual* in the grass or *sensual* touching family members, but suppose we say going barefoot is a *sexual* experience, or hugging our parents a *sexual* response. We carry in our upbringing as well as in this vocabulary very definite ideas of delineation and restriction.

I, at least, have not reached an understanding that totally removes these boundaries and replaces them with my own definitions. However, looking at the subject here, and in our lives and journals, I want to treat sensual awareness as the natural extension of feelings, and limited only by our inhibitions.

Limitations on our physical awareness begin in a psychic circle extending beyond our bodies five to six feet. We tend to live enclosed in shells of inviolate space and are trained to raise our guard at any encroachment upon this personal territory. In the increasingly smaller physical spaces in which many of us live, these private territories are violated constantly and throw us into a state of tension whether or not we are aware of it. And when someone encroaches onto our territory—even benevolently—we often avoid breaking our shells and reaching out to touch and respond. We end up censoring our perceptions in order to protect this psychic bubble. We suffer from this censoring. To explore our sensuality, we must often begin again with the basic awareness of ourselves as bodies within a physical environment.

Remember days on the beach when the sand was so hot it was like walking in ankle-high ovens? Remember sitting so high in the apple tree that the wind took us, limb and all, in its sway? Remember the first snowfall of the year when the negative of November switches over to black on white? Remember the taste of hot fresh bread and honey, and how half the loaf disappeared before we noticed? Remember the first time we kissed someone and knew the softness of other lips? Remember?

Well, I remember. And I write it down in all its

glorious celebratory detail. Sensuality is an awareness that comes giggling and skipping out of the natural inner child. Sensuality is a sense of wonder. There are ways to use the journal to raise again our awarenesss and celebration of senses. If we are separated from such perceptions we may ask:

- What do I see, hear, feel, taste, smell right now?
- How aware am I usually of each sense? Which gets the most attention?
- Where is my body touching the environment right now?
- What did I observe sensually about the people I met today?
- Who and what and how did I touch today? What response did I get?
- What did I eat for lunch? Did I taste it?
- What details do I notice first when walking into a new environment?
- What do I notice first about other people? And what do I think they notice first about me?
- What is happening to the trees today?
- What would my house feel like if I were a cat?

The list is infinite. And it gets more and more playful as we reconnect with the excitement of the world's sensual treasures.

In my own journey to reconnect with sensuality I once experimented with a prolonged fast that brought awareness of my body into new focus.

Journal entry: 2 April 1970
When I woke this morning my first impression was that I have hip bones. I could feel them against the hard mattress and pushed them down excitedly. And I was naked. I remember last night tearing off my nightgown, wanting to be closer to the smooth coolness of the eiderdown.

I notice so many things. My fingernails are long and growing. This tiny phenomenon fascinates me. I can feel the wax in my ears shifting, almost my hair growing. I stand on a chair by the sink just to look at my body. I inspect my back, my buttocks, where I am fatty, where I am skinny. I am losing weight from the top half of my body, making my breasts smaller; my ribs show. But it is a process of detachment and determination. I want to sketch this body because it is suddenly a mystery. I feel my body is a house, a part of the instrument. I am bringing my body into involvement with where my mind is heading.

The fast feels good. Tea with milk is an elixir which succours me. And all the body process is brought to simplicity. There is no fussing over what and when to eat. The choice is vitamins and tea, or a bit of milk or juice. It is enough to give me a sense of caring for myself. And an hour later, I have to urinate. I can almost time it; swallow, stomach, intestine, bladder. I am making water, primeval ablution. I feel like an earth mother sometimes and want to run outside the cave and pee on the grass. I resent squatting over an icy plastic and porcelain machine.

I almost fell down the steps this afternoon, taking for granted that I could swing the corner at the top of the stair the way I usually do. I wrenched my ankle and hung suspended by one armpit on the railing while I tried to figure out the miscommunication. I am coming into a new definition between mind and body and I am going to have to learn and relearn some basic relationships.

This relearning of basic relationships has never left me. It brought into focus all the antisensuality messages I was carrying around inside me as a young woman and taught me to refeel my body in the world. Bodies, our individual bodies, are a basic instrument of sensuality. And bodies, individual bodies, are where many of us begin censoring our acceptance of ourselves and our environment.

Most recently it was the women's movement that raised awareness of the almost universal sense of disgust women have for their bodies. We have been over this thought so many times, shared it with so many women and men, reached so many conclusions, it's hard to even think about it anymore. We've done little pieces of work: lost weight, come to accept the size of our breasts and hips, gotten out a mirror and examined our genitals, but it is still true that a female body is not considered beautiful in this culture unless it matches popular fantasy figures. And deep down in our hearts many of us still tremblingly compare our bodies with that image.

And men? I've always assumed I'd take them any way they came. Only women have to be physically perfect to merit a relationship. But men have told me similar stories of their body anxieties: afraid their chests are too feminine, their legs too bony, their genitals too small, their acne too bad. Too bad . . . for us all. For unless we believe we are beauty-full, we hesitate to touch others and be touched in return. To be ecstatic about the world around us we must perceive ourselves as ecstatic creatures. We must allow ourselves to experience ecstasy. Hiding within bodies we distrust and condemn separates us from this spontaneity. To really accept the beauty of the world, we must have a place in ourselves that understands our own beauty, that accepts the experience of beauty and ecstasy from within. In the journal we start the process of admitting to having a relationship with our bodies.

In my teenage journal I constantly fantasied becoming an actress, and made occasional references to new hair styles and diet. But I never admitted the depth of despair at not conforming to the images in girls' magazines. I never admitted the inner image of myself as ugly and deformed, though I let it alter my social behavior for almost a decade. It wasn't until I was twenty-five that I could admit the energy drain and emotional cost of this fixation on supposed perfection and let my own beauty emerge.

To sit inside our skins and reexplore our body images reveals many messages that may still be operating within us.

- Where did I learn my body image?
- How did Mother feel about her body?
- How did Father feel about his body?
- What family rules did we live by regarding touching, affection, nudity, sex?
- What was the family vocabulary for parts of the body, bodily functions, sexual acts? What did these words imply for us?
- How did I get touched as a child and by whom?
- Were there traumatic instances connected to my early sexual awareness? Have I worked to resolve them?

And looking at the present we ask:

- Am I getting touched in places and ways with which I do not feel comfortable?
- Am I not getting touched in places and ways that I want to be?

- Can I see the source of my comfort and discomfort with certain parts of my body, and being touched there?
- What am I going to do about getting my touching needs met when I know what I want?
- How do I want to reach out to others that is different from my present behavior?

Once we are grounded in understanding ourselves the world opens up around us. In the journal we move again and again from the inner to the outer, reunifying ourselves with the intricate sensuality that surrounds us.

In flow writing we may explore again this sense of wonder, conjuring up fantasies about ant hills, recording the touch of evergreen boughs, watching a candle burn down to its base, perceiving the subtle daily changes in weather . . . CELEBRATING:

Journal entry: 1 July 1975
Another true story about July is that blueberries are among the world's greatest inventions. My tongue sticking out purple, I try to look cross-eyed at it the way I did when I was five. Compromise: on the morning I eat blueberries I wear blue to work. Blue blouse, with my brown arms sticking out like branches, and a blue skirt of all shades folding its cotton comfort around me. And all day I remind myself of breakfast—blueberries!

On the sidewalks of my hill a thousand tiny fading
blossoms are lying face up in the rain. My heart
catches. I am not ready to let the lilacs go by
though they fall and brown as carelessly as they
came, bursting one by thousands into visible
fragrance.

I am disconsolate not to have lived in the alley,
camped out with my Chinese quilt and a pot of
English tea, playing most purple songs all night
on dulcimer and recorder. I am remorseful not
to have plumbed their excuse to be excessive, to
weep great tears, to laugh giddily letting the
whole scheme of things strike me as ridiculous, to
dance Dionysian madness on all the winter's
bones. Lilacs—lilacs—these were my grapes and
wine, and nothing else the ripe year offers for
drink is quite as sweet.

But I have drunk them, motif of my coming
down, coming home to center again. Lilacs
led me to some goodbyes, to some hellos, led me
in and out of old love's longing. And Friday
night I found a bush someone had pruned with
the blossoms still cluster full. I carried home an
armful, set out two huge bouquets and filled my
bed with the rest. Late, after midnight, I lay
naked and luxuriant in my self-created,
self-nurturing bower. The dog sniffed disdainfully
at my romanticism and headed with a sneeze
for the foot of the bed. And I was expecting no

one, just loving the lavender freedom, just loving
myself at midnight.

As our sensuality gets closer to explicit sexuality,
the struggle for perception may deepen, open up areas
of hard, long-ignored feelings.

Journal entry: 19 June 1975

Something on the beach. White, limpid, looking
ocean-logged, inert. Slight movement. In the
pubic seaweed a finger beats the ocean's rhythm
on the sheathed pearl until it shudders. It lives.

First day of my period, first one since April
when I got off the pill. Cramps. I wake and go
through the perfunctory motions of masturbating,
a few mild comes to urge the clots out, to relax
my tense uterus and lower back. I am not turned
on. I am not relating to my sexuality, not relating
to this womanly function. I feel just as I've
described myself—something limpid, squishy,
washed up throbbing on the beach.

And I am angry at MEN. Angry at B.'s intrusion
into last evening and the scent of the hunt that
hangs over him. I am angry at my indiscretion,
telling him the flat above me is vacant. I suddenly
have this image of a huge unwanted prick being
laid over the protected womb of my house. B. is
on the prowl and I don't want the hassle of
having to define boundaries in the household. I
laugh bitterly at my anxiety—controlling bitch!

143

Last week S. sent me his long-promised erotic letter in which he exposes his self-styled free-flowing horniness. I am strangely complimented that he will share its rawness, that he will share the vulnerability attached to his penis.

He says, among other things, that he wants to take all femaleness into his lap and fuck all women. In later conversation I tell him, "It's a different fantasy to be penetrated by mystery rather than your imagined penetration of mystery. If I want to penetrate you, penetrate men or maleness, the only point of entry I have is your head, the way you give me entrance into the spirit of you. The male body does not provide a corresponding genital opening that the woman can take, nor a way to feel her most private part of self being all encompassed, held, accepted in a male vagina."

He laughs—then turns serious and compliments my awareness and sensuality. And we are stuck there again, aware of each other as foreign countries. We sit on opposite ends of the couch like a map of Europe and don't know how to continue the dialogue. Again I feel alone, something tossed up on the beach.

It was several years after I became sexually active, meaning of course that I had sexual intercourse with a man, before I wrote or explored anything more explicit in the journal than the comment, "did it, at last." I never mentioned learning to masturbate at age eleven, petting madly at age seventeen, experimenting with everything but penetration at age twenty. Sex meant "going all the way," not simply enjoying my body with myself or with another body. And "going all the way" implied I was interested in and ready for marriage and monogamous intercourse. The most radical shift I have made from these early experiences has not been a revolution in sexual activities, but an evolution in my willingness to be open about myself as a sexual person. I celebrate my sexuality and take responsibility for my actions, which are grounded in a self-defined sense of honor, respect, and appropriateness. And the journal has been the greatest witness to this growth.

In the journal we may explore, both in direct question asking and in accidental rambling discoveries, our feelings about much of sexuality.

I try out the following thinking in the journal:

- Is there a definite line or a blending between sensuality and sexuality in my feelings? Is this appropriate to my life-style and needs?
- Are there parts of my body where I feel my sexuality is focused?
- Do I treat these parts differently than the rest of my body?
- How comfortable am I with this system? How could I change it?

- How do I get "turned on"? How do I keep myself from being "turned on"?
- Who is in charge of my sexual feelings? Where did I learn these attitudes?
- What do I usually do with my sexual feelings and do I want to change my response to these feelings?
- Do I have (or feel the need for) friendships where I can share my feelings about sexuality as I discover them in the journal?

Using the journal to explore further I remove all practical restrictions and design my ideal sex-life. One way I found to illustrate this is to draw a line in the journal with the words, "total sexual freedom" at one end and "married monogamy" at the other. I made a blue X where my sexual experience places me on the continuum and a red X where my parental-ethical-societal messages say I am supposed to be. With this before me, what do I assume, or fantasy, are the options in the space between the two X's? What are ways I have compromised and how comfortable am I with myself and these adjustments? It is in the realm between the two X's where most of us live, and struggle to define our sexuality.

At this point, the idea of omnisexuality returns to us in new fullness. Sex is not something confined to the pelvis, but is the flowing of all ourselves toward other selves, toward the sensuality in the world around us. In the journey to understand our responsibility and freedom, omnisexuality opens us to a new sense of what is natural. It includes the total body process and the awareness of life energy. It expresses our desires within an understanding of sex as integration. And when we accept it, our natural eroticism flows more freely in the journal and in our lives.

Journal entry: 5 December 1975
Let us talk now of whales—the haunting plaintive
songs of wombs swimming in maternal seas. I
have a record of their voices recorded in my mind
above the tide lines, beyond the reach of
driftwood penises. Safe. Whales sounding in the
deep grey matter of my most secret self. I do
not deny it. Their song the only voice here, they
sing of poems untranslatable into ordinary
speech. Echoes. Icebergs ride the rhythm,
clitorises turned up to meet the tongues of waves,
bodies hidden beneath the turbulence. We talk
of whales, and the coast of Greenland shudders
into song.

This is a beginning. Our bodies are not ours forever. What a shame it would be to have them and never experience their wealth.

Life equals death, for life is change, and in every change something dies, something ceases to be as it was. Death equals life, for death is change and in every change something new occurs, something that was not before is now. This is the great riddle. Its process moves through our lives constantly. Its process moves through every aspect of the journal.

Death takes many forms: deaths of childhood as we assume adult roles, deaths of friendship and love relationships, deaths of marriages, deaths of the parent–child relationship as our children's definitions of our place in their lives evolve, and deaths of the child–parent relationship as we ask our parents for shared adulthood. We experience the death of certain expectations about ourselves as life molds us in one way or another and we confront limitations in our abilities to grow, to change, to excel in careers. And death comes also to us as death, the final confrontation that emerges out of life's littler deaths. People we love will die before us and people who love us will watch us die. For all these experiences we need to contemplate and accept death, to make a lifelong comrade of it.

And for each death there is a grief we need to acknowledge, to process, and to resolve. Sometimes these transitions are easy, celebratory, but when they are not, an awareness of the dynamics of death and grief helps us recognize and deal with them.

Acceptance of death and grief is an aspect of resolving past experiences through the synthesis process discussed in the section on memory. Acceptance of death and grief is an aspect of the letting go of the hurts in the child-hole as we allow ourselves sadness and comfort in the dialogue between child and adult self. Acceptance of death and grief is an aspect of risk taking in relationships, in time structure and problem solving as we deal with the reality of change and cease to expect permanent solutions. Acceptance of death and grief is an aspect of sensuality as we perceive the great and mysterious mortality in the world around us. Whatever life offers us in the way of deaths, we need to grieve when they occur and to integrate our grieving into our being until the deaths become acceptable parts of our history.

Not all these deaths are easy to perceive. They may not wear the mask of abrupt termination we expect death to wear. Sometimes the only way we may know a death has occurred is through being aware of grief. Learning to perceive the grief process we may learn to decipher the death that is causing it.

Grief consists in three major stages. The first stage is shock, and emotional shock has certain things in common with physical shock, such as the denial of an injury. A man may break his leg and hike down off the mountain before feeling pain. And a widow may make all the funeral arrangements and remain a charming hostess to family and friends before she stands alone, aware at last of her irretrievable loss. A mother may send her last child off to school with much cheer and months later be overwhelmed with confusion at her change of time structure. She is then faced with grief. Her sense of normalcy has been disrupted.

The second stage of grief is an overwhelming sense of consequences and a hypersensitivity to the disruption. We are as yet unable to fit the experience of loss or change into our view of ourselves and our lives. During this time the grieving person goes through periods of inertia, anger, sorrow, and denial of the new situation, and the process is even further complicated by a sense of having been betrayed by the person who died or the situation that changed, or the fact of death itself. Family and friends who do not seem to grieve similarly may be objects of many unresolved feelings.

The last stage of grief is recovery, and it is perhaps the hardest to understand. It is not a lessening of the impact of loss and change, but the *incorporation* of this experience into our lives. We do not get over grief, we walk through it. We cannot fully understand the process of recovery until we have dealt seriously with grief ourselves. Our expectations for recovery that precede the process are very different from the sense of recovery that emerges inside the process. This is true whether we are dealing with transition or literal death.

As we define our recovery we may find ourselves isolated. We emerge from the grieving process as changed people, people who carry the reality of that death and the reality of our grief forward with us into the rest of our lives. While the change is occurring we may temporarily be separated from easy social contact with people who do not understand the grieving process or who have their own expectations for our resolution.

However, in the use of the journal we find a place that will accept all our feelings. In the journal we may reveal the secrets carried in our relationship to that death and work to understand and resolve them. In the journal we find a place that does not impose rules of acceptable behavior, acceptable length of grief, acceptable changes during grief. The journal absorbs our labor of grief with the same depth we grant it in other areas, and grief is observable through the same questioning we have applied to ourselves in other situations.

At such a time the understanding of memory is particularly important. Memories become especially meaningful as part of the grieving process. We have all experienced this. A certain song can trip our minds into intimate contact with an old love affair or some earlier period of our lives. The glimpse of a stranger who reminds us of a dead friend, or lost relationship, can flood us with feeling. We need not be afraid of these responses. As our grief is incorporated into our lives these flashes serve to remind us of the long journey we have traveled.

As our lives move further and further down time from a major grief experience we become aware that no one besides our inner self knows the whole story. We become aware of an awesome process of synthesis moving in our lives, which grief brings sharply into focus. We may still be intimate with people, but we will always carry a level of private understanding of ourselves deeper than we can communicate. And the journal becomes not only a tool for survival but also a statement of survival. It becomes a place in which we acknowledge the special privateness of our being.

Journal entry: 26 May 1973

Suddenly in the rush of B. and D.'s wedding I remember what I felt like on the day J. left me that August. All the intervening time does not shield me from full memory of those twenty-four hours and its impact on my life.

I was their bridesmaid. Last night, long after midnight, I sat on the sleeping porch watching my bride-friend toss in her dreams. And I wept silently into the wedding napkins, feeling myself an estranged older woman keeping watch over the younger, more innocent sister. And today, after the little tears of happiness for their beginning, I am again overwhelmed with the business of my own grief.

Now I am riding the bus back home. My heart is broken open like a red tulip falling apart, exposing the black base to the petals and the

yellow unmet stamen. I cry and cry. It rains and
rains.

I remember myself in love and mourn what I
have become without him. I was a good lover
and poured all I had so bountifully in his direction. Today I relive the shock of suddenly finding
myself a woman alone instead of his partner.
I was so emotionally committed to being at his
side, I cannot absorb that reality ripped from me.

Why is today as hard to live through as all
our other partings? Where are my protections
against this hurt?

Journal entry: 25 August 1975
I spent the evening on the porch with a close
friend. We are planning new activities for
autumn and suddenly I remember, it is just three
years ago that J. left. And I have not been
watching for this anniversary, not anticipated
the annual rolling around of this date: I am
through saying *kaddish* for this man.

And I think: if I had known how unlimited
my life would become beyond that sadness, beyond
that shell where I held myself waiting for his
love, how eagerly I would have gotten under
way with my recovery. And I think: if I had
known how long the path would be, how many
moments of despair it contained, how reluctantly
I would have taken my first step. But thank God
for my faith in life's meaning, and for the growing

sense of ownership for each and every moment,
for claiming my life and letting it penetrate
me with all its mysteries!

For I find today that I can have no question
of my willingness to suffer because I am always
washed ashore in new realms of growth and
consciousness. What a miracle to lie open, to
invite my life to hand me any lesson because I
KNOW it will always be all right. To be able
to invite pain to join in my experience and not
to have to control my life to avoid pain is such
a freedom!

Past midnight I stand at the porch door full of
pensive contentment, letting in the sweet deep
thickness of the August night. I walk through the
house stroking mementos that sing in the dark-
ness. It is a good journey.

We cannot live life over, so whatever deaths are
handed to us must be accepted, walked through, and
resolved. These entries express the grieving and the
processing toward synthesis as death mixes with life
in the flow of the journal.

But death also continues to exist as an ultimate
reality—a rite of finality—as well as intermediate rites
of passage. In a ten-month period in 1973, I experienced the loss of seven friends and acquaintances
through a car accident, murder, heart attack, suicide,
and cancer. I could not process one loss before another
followed. Through the confusion and anguish of that

time I developed a resounding respect for the finality of dying and the power of grief. I needed to remain consciously working on the stages of grief in my journal. This work was complicated by the fact that most of these deaths occurred far away and in only one case was I able to participate in funeral rites. In my loss of the six other friends I had to experience the grief alone. The people in Minneapolis could not share my friends' importance to me, and there was no place in which to carry on the grief process other than the privacy of my thoughts and journal writing. The experience made me acutely aware that I still have many deaths to face that are even closer to my heart and that I need to make peace with death as part of my personal life expectations.

Our cultural response to death is usually very psychically unsettling. We attempt to separate ourselves from intimacy with it and wonder why it haunts us still. We refuse to discuss it in our families and yet are attracted to vicarious experiences with violence that make a myth of death, on television, in books and newspapers, and at the movies. Perhaps more than any other feeling, our reactions to death are the ones we tend to keep most hidden. We are not comfortable with death. We need to know we *can* contemplate death, can experience these feelings, can withstand both thoughts of our own death and the sorrow of another's death.

I saw death for the first time the summer I worked as a hospital nurse's aide. A girl came to the hospital

155

dying of cancer. She handled her last days with such grace, acceptance, and care for her grieving family that I was in awe of her. After she died I went into her room to stand with her a moment and experience my living self beside this twin empty shell. We were both nineteen years old. Death is a reality. But we are so trained to avoid it, perhaps protected, fortunately, from personal experience with it, that sometimes the only way we can comprehend death's power is to stand next to it in fantasy.

Suppose I have just found out I have three months to live. In the journal I deal with this death: I design my illness, decide how to deal with growing incapacity, with different relationships, imagine who and what I need to bid farewell to, how I will structure time, and what projects I will begin or complete.

Journal entry: 21 February 1976
Three months to live! My God, that means I may just hold out until the lilacs come . . . may just survive long enough to feel the rains warm and take us both . . . Take ME! Death take me . . . take me where? How dare it! I'll just be thirty this April. I have plans for his decade. Death take me then!?

The phone jangles in the house as I write, disturbing me. Death is disturbing me. No, I don't believe it or I would storm with rage. You *can't*. I haven't started the book, or finished a

156

hundred other stories. You *can't* snatch time away from me like this!

But you just did, didn't you, Death. Anger, anger, anger, anger—I whirl with tears flinging off my cheeks, smoting the faces of watching friends. Friends who have gathered to help, comfort, try to understand. Who will I tell, who? I want to have company here, don't want to play the strong lady, the silent martyr. I've grown through experiences of others' deaths; they will grow through sharing mine. I make no prediction on the course of my relationships in the next three months.

Three months is not a year, is hardly any time at all. Can't cope with everything, with everyone, or I will have no time left to cope with myself. Must keep space for this most painful lonely task, this is the last three months this self is going to exist.

. . . I want to die at home if possible, if that's not too scary. Want my own room and lilacs, please God bring out the lilacs on time, want the mementos of my life around me, and friends, a few friends who will let go with me, all the pieces accepted.

. . . But wait, that is grief, not death. Death is disengagement. When I get down to that moment, I see I must be allowed, must allow myself, to disengage from life. Hard to imagine that concept now, I cling so tenaciously to life, my self's life funneling out ahead of me with promised time. But I will learn to disengage. By the day I die I will have set myself free of expectations. They will miss me more on that day than I will miss them, for I will have horizons beyond our glances.

. . . NO! I choose life. I want to stay here and explore it with them, not to let go . . . how can I not have the choice anymore? Dying in THREE MONTHS!!!? Fierce, fierce, fierce.

As this entry indicates, it is not hard to find our feelings about death. And once we have worked on the acceptance of death and our experiences of grief and included them in the journal's dialogue, the journal becomes grounded into our lives more deeply than ever before.

And when the journal is grounded into our mortality, into life, and death, we end up writing a vocabulary of change. We sense a great ebb and flow through all we had perceived as sturdy and immutable. And perhaps we are afraid. The solid ground on which we stand is molten at its core. We sense the lacy order of atoms holding the world together. And this whirling dervish of a universe, this constant stage of transformation is all we have. And so change *must be* in the nature of things. If we are seeking a way to conceive of immortality, we can look at it first through this vision of change.

Life equals death because life is change.

Death equals life because death is change.

Change is the constant, the signal for rebirth, the egg of the phoenix. As change moves through our recorded lives it raises its own questions on the nature of the journey and becomes a door through which we glimpse more than mortality. We glimpse a mutable Universe.

In the journey of the journal, beneath all our other struggles, we may reach a point where we wear out the emotional bases for understanding ourselves. We find a point where our capacity for change, our ability to cope with problems, seem exhausted and we fear we have reached the end of the journey. It is the nature of our exploration, of our introspection, concentration, and honesty in the journal, to uncover at last this sense of limitation. We are confronted with the need for a new dimension. There are still many questions that are not answerable with the vocabulary of search we have been using. At this point the journey confronts us with a choice of terminating it or transforming it. How we respond to the proffered openness of a wider universe at this point of outgrowing our present personal universe is a crisis point in the journal. And the crisis raises new questioning:

- Do I believe in "a way through"?
- Do I view life as a journey with some kind of meaning?
- What is the basis for my self-acceptance?
- What is the basis for decisions made about directions, relationships, career goals, psychological change?
- What motivates all my exploration in the journal?

Through these questions we come full circle, returning to the original assumptions for the journal. The first assumption was that *we are capable of having a relationship with our own minds.* In our journal expressions thus far we have built this point of consciousness into our writing and being. We have found the dichotomous relationship a working partner in our growth. The second assumption was that *this relationship is intelligent and basically benevolent.* It encompasses our personal psychology but also opens the awareness and possibility of life's independent longing to evolve. We have become instruments of this longing and at the point where we suspect the end of insight, we may consciously open ourselves to the capacity for overview. The therapeutic nature of the journal is based on this psychic drive for wholeness. A third assumption was that *writing makes the connections within the mind conscious* and frames them in a vocabulary we understand because they are generated by ourselves. Through our writing we have set free in ourselves a conversation of which we had been only partially

160

conscious. The conversation is now revealed to have a life of its own, to have questions of its own. The last assumption was that *this activity, the writing and the journey, is essential.* We may have worked with all these assumptions and still find ourselves in crisis.

At this point where we mourn the limitations to which psychology has brought us, we may find our understanding of psychology transformed within us. The unconscious mind into which we have dipped the journal for revelation is the natural and accessible source of the next dimension. It is the meeting point between mortality and immortality. It is the point at which the emotional quest becomes a visionary quest.

We are writers in a context, and given the context of the journey in our culture it is only natural that the visionary quest will speak to us in a psychological vocabularly. Psychology is the frontier of visions. In psychology we find the transformation and blending of the conscious and unconscious languages, the mortal and immortal voices. Theology speaks of "holiness" and psychology speaks of "whole-ness." Theology speaks of "atonement" and psychology speaks of "at-one-ment." Theologists speak of the "fear of the Lord" and psychologists speak of the "respect for the Self." There is no real separation between these vocabularies, and there is no real limitation to the work of the journey. We arrive again at Graves's truth—"There is one story only."

Robert Jay Lifton, in his work *Boundaries: Psycho-*

logical Man in Revolution [1] elucidates this point of arrival and departure as we are confronted in the journal with mortality and immortality.

> . . . I would claim that man *requires* a sense of immortality in the face of inevitable biological death. This sense of immortality need not be merely a denial of the fact of his death, though man is certainly prone to such a denial. It also represents a compelling, universal urge to maintain an inner sense of continuity, over time and space, with the various elements of life. This sense of immortality is man's way of experiencing his connection with all of human history.

Lifton elaborates on this sense by exploring five modes of immortality. He sees first the biological mode in which we sense our lives continuing in and through the lives of our children, finding comfort in the continuity of generations. Secondly, we see immortality in a theological sense, as expressed in various religions concerning life after death. This is the spiritual conquest of death. A third mode is that which is achieved through our works, the creative products of our lives that survive us. Certainly the creative impetus in journal writing supports this need for concrete evidence of having existed. A fourth mode is achieved by the sense of the survival of nature, to incorporate the world of time, space, and stars that will long outlive us. And

1. New York: Random House, 1970.

162

the fifth mode is that of mysticism, experiencing moments of transcendence in which the reality of death disappears in a higher state of rapture. Lifton concludes his examination of modes with this remark:

> . . . What I am suggesting then is that the symbolic modes of immortality are not merely problems one ponders when dying. They are constantly perceived inner standards, though often indirect and outside awareness, by which we evaluate our lives, by which we maintain feelings of connection, significance, and movement so necessary to everyday psychological existence.

It is my belief this point of confrontation is always before us and within us, and surfaces naturally out of the inner journey. In this connection to immortality we are not necessarily looking through the portals of organized religion, or the prejudices of our religious upbringings, or even the popularization of the Judeo-Christian heritage. We are talking about a moment of transforming enthrallment. This moment is when the self of the journal meets the self beyond the journal. It is the moment when we recognize that the journey of the self is the journey to the self. We have been journeying after ourselves and discover the journey to the self is the journey that leads us into the Universe.

For centuries the writers of journals have reached this point of revelation and written it down in wonder. Despite the messages of materialistic society, that in maturity we outgrow the need for religion, the seeking in the journal reopens the doors of mystery within us. Human beings of the twentieth century, for all their technical sophistication, are still beings in search of the self, the larger whole, their spirituality. The voice that speaks out of us, and to us, is the immortal voice.

Journal entry: 25 January 1971

Once I read of a little boy who had cancer in his eyes and had to have them surgically removed. His parents took him to many beautiful places, through parks and gardens, to see sailing boats, and to the zoo. And they filled his mind with such wondrous sights.

And I am thinking it is time for all of us to take the hands of children and lovers and to say good-bye to so much we are destroying in our times. I am full of weeping, and recognize my great unfaithfulness in this despair. I know this labyrinth well, and I am learning. . . .

I am learning to let the Universe be free of my definitions for its survival. I am learning to let life be free of my definitions and to accept the inrushing sound of the Universe singing its own unfoldment. I believe it. I believe you Shepherd Universe. The "I" in me just doesn't want to die. Little "I" has such trembling expectations of mortality, but bigger "I" has such a tunnel of vision beyond my understanding. Bigger "I" perceives the continuance, never quite

164

in focus, but moving within me and without me. The rivers of little "I" and bigger "I" converge and bring me their gifts of restlessness and peace.

The need to acknowledge change began this journey, became the motif of the journal, and now frames our final awareness of the journey. Change is the constant and we are constantly in change. To cease trembling before this awareness, to absorb it in our perceptions from the first entrance into the journal's pages, is the great gift that awaits our faith. To stand at the point of termination and allow our journey and ourselves to be transformed is the most private and important work the journal will ever accomplish.

Emblazoned in my mind is a quote from T.S. Eliot's *Four Quartets*:

> We shall not cease from exploration
> And the end of all our exploring
> Will be to arrive where we started
> And know the place for the first time.

Writing On from Here

I cannot write too long in the perspective of the Universe or I fall into it, seduced by my enthrallment, rolling weightless in inner space with my pen helpless in my hand. So I keep a star-hole in my pocket where I slip the Universe for safekeeping. Strange how infinity can become a pocket-sized awareness. I ponder it in the simple miracles that are around me always. I wonder about things:

- How do orange slices hold together all their intricate membranes?

- How many buttons are being made today around the world? Who is making them and what are they thinking about as they bend over the machine?
- How small are the capillaries in a mouse's paw, and what spark of energy keeps the tiny heart beating?
- How many hands touched the postcard I got from France? Do they care at all for the messages that pass through their fingers?
- What signals the maple leaf's turning? And where does the red color come from that creeps up the stem?
- How does my dog really see the world? Do his eyes register an impression of—squirrel—the same way mine do, or are we looking at two different animals?
- What is a photograph?

There are miracles enough to astound me for a lifetime and to provide me a place of perspective and grounding in my own small visions. I pocket the star-hole because I have something very ordinary, very over-the-coffee-cup and practical left to say.

This book has been a process of spiraling down from first considerations of paper, pen, and privacy to later considerations of life and death. And I want to say again that this is a very ordinary journey. The journal entries at the beginning and end of the book are similar in style, insight, and exploration. In a way this is a journey without differentiation—the miracle is everywhere. The miracle does not exist so much in what we contemplate, but that we contemplate at all. The hardest miracle of life is growing into consciousness: What to do with that consciousness is to celebrate our wonder and amazement. The most miraculous aspect of the journal is that it exists, and the most miraculous aspect of the journey is that we perceive it.

Most of journal writing and most of this book is an encouragement to reach deeper and deeper into the process of the miracle. We have been together on a seduction. The Latin *seducere* means to lead in, and the journal seduces us day by day into the core of writing and awareness. We can get so far into the journal that we become the journal, become the river that flows out of consciousness onto the banks of our blank pages. This is an enthralling place to be, but it is not the complete journey.

The Latin *educare* means to lead out, and the journal also needs to educate us, to let us pull back and perceive the product of our writing. The educational nature of the journal lies first in the initial introspection, from which we somehow learn, and then in turning over the subjectivity of introspection and viewing it objectively. We need both processes—the inward and the outward. The journal calls for a procedure of life review. Some of this life review is incorporated in the introspection process by including personal agendas, the interpretation of dreams, and the division of our lives into manageable volumes of writing and time.

171

When I set aside time to consciously review my journal work I start by asking myself:

- · What do I remember is in the journal since I last looked?
- · What do I think are the main themes, ideas, major questions, and most important feelings and discoveries?

Then on some special day, like New Year's or my birthday or the day I complete a journal notebook or face a major change in life, I take time to review the journal. Sometimes I make a code for myself to stick at the top corner of pages so I can quickly find entries on specific subjects.

P = parents C = Chrissie, c = child-hole,
A = anger, L = literature—prose passages that
might lead to stories or poems, L G = life goals,
D = dreams, D I = dream interpretation, and
various initials indicate references to people in
the text.

In rereading I apply the questions I asked myself while writing. I look for the secrets, the imbalance, the issues I am including and the issues I am leaving out. I notice the complex synchronism, the way so many things surface and flow through the journal all at the same time. I cull perceptions from my recorded life as though I were reading a novel and appreciating the characters and plot of each chapter. I become my audience. And I pause to acknowledge and celebrate the contents.

It seems natural here to mention Anaïs Nin and Ira Progoff, whose works with the journal have contributed to the way we perceive and value the personal voice.

Dr. Progoff, a psychotherapist trained in Jungian analysis and depth psychology, has developed a method of journal keeping called "journal feedback" and the use of a specifically designed psychological notebook called the "intensive journal." Progoff's main concern is to bring depth contact with our inner selves into our daily lives, and to codify a system of reach and return that we may use individually and consistently. He sees the dichotomous relationship as central to this process. Much of the intensive journal is written in dialogue, and the dialogues are grounded in the personal experience of our deep center. Journal feedback is provided through a system of cross-referencing entries that are written in nineteen carefully defined journal sections.

Progoff's concept of the journal as a psychological notebook and his tight structure of writing and personal life-appraisal are different in style and method from the materials presented here, but certainly compatible in intent. I have avoided dealing with some methods of dialogue and referencing not out of disagreement, but out of respect for his development of these ideas. I believe the work of the journal can be as full and well understood by writers with or without confining the writing process to Progoff's structural format. Writers who find the need for more structure or wish to pursue a greater understanding of the role of structure and review in journal writing should seek out Progoff's material. Progoff communicates his work through weekend journal workshops held around the nation and in his recently published book, *At a Journal Workshop*.[2] The book and workshop information are available through Dialogue House Associates, 80 East 11 Street, New York, New York 10011.

In structure, Anaïs Nin represents the other end of the spectrum. Her voluminous diary writing, now published in five volumes covering the years of her life from 1931 to 1955, expresses a rich literary style of undifferentiated energy, perception, and personal relationship to the world. She includes her intellectual and educational growth, her experiences as a therapist and a client in therapy, dialogues of her relationships to the famous and non-famous, dreams, story and novel ideas, descriptive prose, and her deep emotional thoughts. In her book on the writing process, *The Novel of the Future*,[3] Chapter 5 is called "The Genesis of the Diary." Here she reveals the diary as the source of all other writing, and credits it with the honesty she needs to grow. She says, "Another aspect of notebook or diary writing is that it records a pilgrim's progress of the artist at work. I worked out my problems as a woman writer, as a writer of poetic fiction,

2. New York: Dialogue House Library, 1975.
3. New York: MacMillan-Collier Books, 1968.

within the diary." She adds, "The diary, dealing always with the immediate present, the warm, the near, being written in white heat, developed a love of the living moment, of the emotional reaction to experience which revealed that powers of re-creation lie in the senses rather than in memory or critical, intellectual observation." Such a philosophy behind her work both as a novelist and diarist has contributed significantly to the acceptance of journal writing as a literary genre, and has heightened our awareness of the journal's importance in psychological growth and understanding.

Because Progoff and Nin are articulate and published writers, they provide a focal point for understanding the potential in the journal. But they do not represent this potential—we do. We all, individually, contribute our own energy and uniqueness to the journal. And in every journal a new journey is conceived and traveled. The journal is *our* book. The journal is *our* psychology. The journal is *our* literature. We are the intimate and we are the whole. We fill the silent spaces with a lovely sound of pens scratching on blank pages. And this energy is never lost, it rises out of the situations and solitudes in which we write and provides a bond of activity and awareness to support us all. We can take courage from this bond whether or not we share our writings.

We write journals and leave our lives like letters in the earth. No approach to journal writing should end without reaffirming that connection to the self and to the community we each intimately express.

Journal entry: Autumnal Equinox 1976
Today I finished the book. It was on Midsummer's Eve that I moved my life to the kitchen table, piled it with journal volumes, papers, resource books and various drafts. I have spent the summer attached to my creative mess by an umbilicus of words and I am exhausted. Wherever I rest my hands I leave inky fingerprints of blue smudges. I feel drained of words. The book has taken them all, like a child suckling me dry. Now I want to pick it up and shake it.

"Enough of your demands on my energy and time, on my creativity and journey. Go outside and play. Make your own friends. Fight your own battles with the neighborhood kids. Stand on your own. I will be here again at sundown, to tuck you in, but I have given you all I can give you this day."

I stand by the post box at midnight, dropping manuscript pages into its gaping blue mouth. A candle is lit in the window, and I turn up the block toward home. And the journal, oh my own journal, private again, no longer poked and prodded for examples of this or that, waits open on the clean and polished desk.

Appendix: Journal Seminars

Many of the thoughts and exercises presented here are being used as guidelines for exploring the journal during eight-week journal seminars. Members of a seminar come together one evening a week to share responses to previous work, discuss topics the coming week, and take home new guidelines for work. Group response indicates that this guided "journal support group" is very helpful to the writing process and the encouragement of inner dialogue. It provides a place to share successes and air gripes, to overcome fears and get over writing blocks. It provides a context in which to nurture each other.

It is also apparent that one week is not long enough to probe in depth many of the questions raised, nor that all personal writing between meetings is on the week's topic. Therefore many groups have spontaneously organized followup sessions, approximately a month after the seminar ended, to share further insights and experiences as people worked independently, and to continue a supportive community focused on journal writing. The informal Journal Club, made up of people from several groups, meets monthly in members' homes to share journal entries and chat about journal keeping. These meetings are a social gathering usually having a prearranged topic for reading, with open readings toward the end of the evening. There is no pressure for members to share their writings.

As the seminars have proved supportive and exciting to so many people, I include here some opening assumptions from these group experiences for anyone interested in using these materials within a journal group. Groups have usually consisted of around fifteen people, sessions two hours in length.

My opening assumptions as group facilitator include:

· Everyone present has been, or is interested in, keeping a journal.
· There is a commitment to session attendance for a specified number of weeks.
· There is a commitment to write during the week.
· There is understanding that the writing outlines

are *not* assignments, and will not be turned in nor the contents of work revealed beyond what each writer wishes to freely share in the group. Both the group members and the facilitator will respect each individual's privacy.

· Beyond personal privacy in writing, there is also the understanding of confidentiality within the group regarding things shared in sessions. The attitude of the group is not to analyze one another, but to support every other person's growth and self-exploration and to remain nonjudgmental.

· The group experience is open to evolution as needs arise, and each member is responsible for stating her needs and getting the fullest experience possible for herself from group sessions.

Part of the experiment of writing this book has been to translate material from predominantly spoken group expressions onto the page. But friends who have used the book in manuscript form report their comfort with the book in private. By its very nature journal writing is an activity of solitude. These ideas were first found in the solitude of the writing experience and rest well in that situation. While some insights may be shared, the journey we are undertaking remains at its heart a solitary pilgrimage. The journal itself is the friend who most deeply supports, guides, and follows us, and our basic alliance must remain within the trustworthy boundaries of our writing.

Bibliography

This bibliography is not a list of journals. It is a totally eclectic and personally chosen smattering of resources that have spoken to me in the course of my thinking about the processes involved in this book. These resources are simply other writers' explorations into the journey that have added to my own thinking and are grouped basically by topic.

According to James Cummings, antiquarian book dealer and collector, there are about 9,000 journals and diaries in print. He should know, for he probably has the most thorough annotated collection in the country—about 7,800 volumes. This collection resides with him in a special room of his Victorian house in Stillwater, Minnesota.

But for those of us too far away to journey into the wonder of that room of recorded lives, the public library is the next best resource for finding published diaries. Looking under the heading *Diary* in the card catalogs of each of many city libraries, I have found several hundred volumes available. I have also found library systems responsive to public demand, and that as people request journals and material regarding journals, libraries are willing to add to their collections.

Considerations for Blank Pages

NIN, ANAIS, *The Novel of the Future.* New York: Macmillan-Collier, 1968.

PLIMPTON, GEORGE, ed. *Writers at Work: The PARIS REVIEW Interviews.* Series 1–3. New York: The Viking Press. 1967.

PROGOFF, IRA. *At a Journal Workshop.* New York: Dialogue House Library, 1975.

———. *The Symbolic and the Real.* New York: McGraw-Hill, 1963.

MOFFAT, JANE, and PAINTER, CHARLOTTE. *Revelations: Diaries of Women.* New York: Random House, 1974.

Memory

DE BEAUVOIR, SIMONE. *Memoirs of a Dutiful Daughter.* Cleveland and New York: World, 1959.

JUNG, CARL G. *Memories, Dreams and Reflections.* New York: Random House-Vintage, 1961.

NIN, ANAIS. *Seduction of the Minotaur.* Chicago: Swallow Press, 1961.

The Child Within

COOPER, DAVID. *The Death of the Family.* New York: Random House-Vintage, 1970.

HARDING, M. ESTHER. *The Parental Image: Its Injury and Reconstruction.* New York: G. P. Putnam, 1965.

LAING, R. D. *The Politics of the Family and Other Essays.* New York: Random House-Vintage, 1969.

SATIR, VIRGINIA. *Peoplemaking.* Palo Alto: Science and Behavior Books, 1972.

Dreams, Twilight Images, and Fantasy

FARADAY, ANN. *Dream Power.* New York: Coward, McCann and Geoghegan, 1972.

————. *The Dream Game*. New York: Harper & Row, 1974.

FROMM, ERICH. *The Forgotten Language: An Introduction to the Understanding of Dreams, Fairy Tales and Myths*. New York: Grove Press, 1951.

GARFIELD, PATRICIA. *Creative Dreaming*. New York: Simon and Schuster, 1974.

MAHONEY, MARIA F. *The Meaning in Dreams and Dreaming: The Jungian Viewpoint*. Secaucus, N.J.: Citadel Press, 1966.

PERLS, FREDERICK S. *Gestalt Therapy Verbatim*. Lafayette, Calif.: Real People Press, 1969.

Friendship

LAIR, JESS. *I Ain't Well, But I Sure Am Better*. New York: Doubleday, 1975.

STEINBERG, DAVID, and DILLWORTH, ANN. *Yellow Brick Road: Steps Toward a New Way of Life*. Ben Lomand, Calif.: Red Alder Press, 1974.

Time Structuring and Problem Solving

JAMES, MURIEL, and JONGEWARD, DOROTHY. *Born to Win: Transactional Analysis with Gestalt Experiments*. Reading, Mass.: Addison-Wesley, 1971.

KOBERG, DON, and BAGNALL, JIM. *The Universal Traveler*. Los Altos, Calif.: William Kaufman, 1972.

ROGERS, CARL, and STEVENS, BARRY. *Person to Person: The Problem of Being Human*. Lafayette, Calif.: Real People Press, 1967.

Sensuality and Sexuality

BARBACH, LONNIE GARFIELD. *For Yourself: The Fulfillment of Female Sexuality*. New York: Doubleday, 1975.

DOWNING, GEORGE. *The Massage Book*. New York: Random House-The Bookworks, 1972.

ROZNAK, BETTY, and ROZNAK, THEODORE, eds. *Masculine/Feminine*. New York: Harper-Colophon, 1969.

RUSH, ANNE KENT. *Getting Clear—Body Work for Women*. New York and Berkeley: Random House-The Bookworks, 1972.

Mortality

DILLARD, ANNIE. *Pilgrim at Tinker Creek*. New York: Harper Magazine Press, 1974.

DUNNE, JOHN S. *Time and Myth: A Meditation on Storytelling As an Exploration of Life and Death*, Garden City, N.Y.: Doubleday, 1973.

185

ROSS, ELIZABETH KUBLER. *On Death and Dying*. New York: Macmillan, 1969.

Immortality

BENDER, TOM. *Environmental Design Handbook*. New York: Schocken Books, 1976.

ELIADE, MIRCEA. *Rites and Symbols of Initiation: The Mysteries of Birth and Rebirth*. New York: Harper, 1958.

JEFFERS, ROBINSON. *Not Man Apart*. San Francisco: Sierra Club Books; New York: Ballantine, 1965.

JUNG, CARL G. *Man and His Symbols*. Garden City, N.Y.: Doubleday, 1964.

LILLY, JOHN C. *The Center of the Cyclone: An Autobiography of Inner Space*. New York: Julian Press, 1972.

MARTIN, P. W. *Experiment in Depth*. London: Routledge and Kegan Paul, 1955.